The
GROWING
of a
ROSE

REBUILDING *and* RESTORING
LIFE AFTER TRAUMA

SUSAN H. BARR

FREILING
PUBLISHING

Published by Freiling Publishing,
a division of Freiling Agency, LLC.

70 Main Street, Suite 23-MEC
Warrenton, VA 20186

www.FreilingPublishing.com

Library of Congress Control Number: 2019918302

ISBN 9781950948178

Printed in the United States of America

Foreward

"I met Susan in high school. She was a popular, "life-of-the-party" cheerleader. She usually occupied the "center of attention" position in any room-the territory I painfully avoided. As a shy nerdy trombone-player, I preferred the back row in the "center of obscurity "zone. Yet, despite our polarized roles in the strata of adolescent culture, I was drawn to her heart. Not in a romantic way. Rather, as a newly surrendered follower of Jesus, I sensed His compassion for the heart of this unbridled filly. Amid the laughter and the banter that frequently surrounded Susan, her heart would bleed through. It was a good heart. A sincere heart. A hungry heart longing for all that is true and real and lasting. It was also a broken heart, crying out for the healing love only the Great Physician can bring.

Susan's quest for more took her in many directions, some of them excruciatingly painful. Wherever she searched she held nothing back. She tells her story with the same uninhibited candor.

As I read this book, I experienced a tsunami of emotions. Tears. Laughter. Passion. Pain. And in the end, loads of joy. This woman lives with a heart wide open-a heart now filled with the overwhelming love of the Lover of our souls."

Dave Hess
Sr. Pastor
Christ Community
Camphill, PA

Dedication

I dedicate this book first and foremost to Jesus Christ and His glory and next to all those who have spoken truth by Holy Spirit into my being for freedom's sake, enabling Him to fully realize within me the one I was created to be. The journey: experiences, prayers, books, encouragement, even difficulties have all played out in the plan of His salvation and freedom. So, if the Son set you free, you will be free indeed. John 6:36 NIV

Thank you all for being a part of His story of my life.

Table of Contents

Prologue

Friday, October 11, 2019, 2:15 am

I am having trouble falling asleep, I think a late cup of coffee yesterday morning and excitement are the reasons, so I quietly climbed the staircase into the living room where my journal awaited my company. Writing to me is cathartic. I have always enjoyed putting pen to paper and still prefer it over computer. Whether it was writing letters to pals from church camp, forming a poem, drawing an artistic creation, or journaling my thoughts. Allowing my inner being freedom of expression, unknowingly was a cherished companion. With me since youth and steadfastly staying with me through thick and thin, tough and very tough, happy and sad, lucid and confused, and Loved and unloved, days, nights and even very early mornings.

Just recently on a two-day respite to the beach, Joni, my best sister and close friend, chortled when I said I need to write something on my calendar, in lieu of using my phone. She thinks my habit odd in the day of smartphones. She uses her phone as her secretary and Me; I write it down with a faithful pen in a bound calendar: recording and keeping details that encapsulate the minutes forming hours in my days, words that define eventful times, experiences and relationships. She does know though it is a part of who I am, and I am not giving it up.

Since I have finished my book, the one God has been writing and planning for this very season, I have noticed a marked difference of increase in the flow of my words to my pen and an enjoyment forming thoughts into sentences that seem more descriptive. My journaling seems matured and at 63 (don't tell anyone), reveals a lifelong love between me, my script and the story we must write for the herald to run with it. Tom, my publisher, sent me that verse yesterday morning for encouragement. Habakkuk 2:2 New International Version Then the Lord replied: "Write down the revelation and make it plain on tablets that a herald may run with it." Tom is my herald. The sense of expectation of birthing my book, after many years of its forming within me, is beyond my realm of experience. But next week as the contract comes to fruition, I will step into the fulfillment of God's last days plans for my life here on earth. I believe he told me many years ago that I would be one of the generation that would not die a physical death but would see Him coming in the clouds, surrounded by His glory. But first a mission…

I am so glad He saved me from my troubles and revealed His love for me so I could be healed, grow, and become His Bride: A rose of His creation, revealing His beauty and fragrance to a world who has forgotten "to stop and smell the roses". Please Stop, you'll be glad you did!

Love because He first loved me,
Susan Jo Hartman Bar

Contact me through AmericanButyRose@gmail.com.

Jimmy Nimon

…" Scholars may miss Jesus and a prostitute find Him.
A prostitute may be looking in all the wrong places,
but at least she is looking for love.

Jimmy Nimon
Sr. Pastor
Lifeway Church
Lebanon, PA

CHAPTER 1 ❧

What kind of hybrid do you want?

"A THORN DEFENDS THE ROSE, HARMING ONLY
THOSE WHO WOULD STEAL ITS BLOSSOM."

WEBSTER'S DICTIONARY defines hybrid: an offspring of two
different races, breeds, varieties, species or genera. We are included
in this definition when we are born. Inside each of us is the DNA
of God along with His potential desire for our being; each of us
unique in design and purpose dwelling in the fleshly body given to
us by our earthly parents. Healthy growth requires food: Physical,
emotional and spiritual foods to be offered by mother and father
within their understanding of their foundational elements for
human make-up. All nourishment enriches growth until we reach
the age and ability to choose for ourselves to become His intended
creation or not. The foundations given to us as children are most
often weak, cracked, broken and in some cases non-existent;
influencing our life decisions in ways we often do not recognize.
This lack of insight overshadows our identity and understanding
of the One who sends us forth to be a force for Love in the world.
However, from our entrance into the world, our experiences are

flawed and require His intervention to realize His design and our identity.

As a child, I was raised in a home with both parents and three brothers, two older and one younger. Our family seemed successful, in our small community, and it was in some ways but not in all. Father and mother were a handsome couple. Father was born of Germanic heritage, a native of the same community, born in a Mill farmhouse, by a stream, which still stands today. Mother was a European Mixed descent of English, French, Irish, and Norwegian, born a year after father in 1924, in a larger PA city, moving to the community her junior year of high school. Both were one of seven children. My father, the eldest, raised by both parents until age eleven, when his father was taken from the family by typhoid fever. The youngest daughter, Mother's parents lived well into her adult years. Daddy had two brothers and four sisters and mother had two sisters and four brothers. Father was raised in the Catholic tradition and mother within the Lutheran traditions of the Christian Faith.

Father always recounted seeing her in physics, his thought the first time: "I am going to marry that girl!" 5'3", long blonde hair and sky-blue eyes with a beautiful smile to highlight a fun-loving personality attracted his attention. Dad was a more serious sort but, his handsome face, dark hair and determination made him very attractive, personable, and likely to succeed at whatever he wanted to accomplish.

The Great Depression greatly shaped the souls of its generation: followed by a world war that determined, at least for a season, my parent's choices. Father enlisted in the Army and went to Germany to fight becoming a prisoner of war (POW) in

German territory the final five- and one-half months of the war
in 1945. After his capture, he was treated with some privilege for
the fact that he spoke German and could interpret for his captors.
However, conditions were non the less difficult including nine- or
ten-hour workdays, six days a week, with Sundays for barracks
clean up, haircuts, or even card games. Rations never changed
from meager dark sourdough bread, a little marmalade and coffee
for breakfast and a second evening meal of barley and potato soup
and sometimes rarely a minute amount of meat. Coffee was made
from roasted barley.

Most slept in barracks of thirty to thirty-five men, however,
the privilege my father received was to sleep in one of only six. He
was walking point the day he was captured and released in the end
weighing only 115 lbs. for his 5'9" frame. Upon his return to the
US he received rest and relaxation with other soldiers in upstate
NY for some weeks.

Mother's career choice took her to Philadelphia Lankanau
School of Nursing to complete the Registered Nursing program
of three years. On weekends sometimes, father and she enjoyed
times together in the city, after his return. New Year's Eve 1947 he
proposed marriage. September 6, the same year, they were joined
in marriage in the Lutheran church and one year and six days later
they became parents of a son.

Dad worked hard from the age of twelve, using skills learned
as a teenage apprentice to a local shoe repairman. Opening his
own shop in town, and training his two younger brothers, while
Mom kept the home front with all the responsibilities of wife and
mother. Two years later brought the arrival of a second son. An
eventual job change took dad on the road daily with International

Shoe Machine Co. as a sales/service rep while selling Cutco Cutlery in his evenings provided extra income to make about $50 a week.

A large house encompassing a half of a block was purchased, including two attached apartments which generated income. One my father lived in as a young man with his widowed mother and siblings. Including two attached apartments generated income and the land allowed for a large productive garden and included two fruitful pear trees gracing the yard. The fruit was delicious, but I could have done without the wasps.

I loved evenings digging rich dark soil in the garden, picking and tasting fresh snap beans, sugar peas and black raspberries, during the harvest season. Our neighborhood was bustling with a liberal arts college, a coal business, shoe factory, the railroad station, and a tack shop, on our favorite sledding hill, above and across the railroad tracks. In the summer the Tack Shop was the location of horse shows and the 4-H Fair. And in winter, Mr. Heisey the owner, could sometimes be seen driving his horse-drawn sleigh on the snow-covered streets through town.

Spring's arrival, with signs of the season, flowers in bloom, green leaves budding, grass bursting from the hardened winter grounds softened by spring rain; all their fragrances filled the air, when I was born in May of 1956. Eight years had passed, since my parent's union, family life with two sons was well established and my arrival on the scene a big disruption to the status quo. Not only had time passed, but also scheduling changes, acceptance and relational adjustments (both physical and emotional) occurred because I was a first-born girl; a daughter, sister and Daddy's little girl. From my arrival and far into adulthood I would have to fight to find my identity. My struggle to feel loved and know where I fit into family was ever present. Letters my mother had received and kept revealed feelings of competition and jealousy wreaking relational havoc in our family way into the future.

Daily coffee klatch among the neighborhood during summer break gave plenty of playtime opportunity away from parental supervision. Children were free to run the gamut of surrounding streets and alleyways, playing games of hide and seek, tag, or swinging to the tunes of the day as we sang the words we could recall. At times wandering blocks from home to collect leaves, acorns, and maple seedpods. Finding fun sticking them on our noses to look silly and laugh, was a simple way of enjoying life. When we adventured from the home block, we often visited the college science lab looking in amazement at the specimens frozen in time in formaldehyde. Our favorite scary one was a two headed snake. Part of the fun was entering the building on the sly, unsure whether we would be welcomed, hiding from anyone who might chase us from the building. Though the freedom from supervision gave way for inappropriate behavior and long-lasting implications for getting away with those behaviors.

Our adult lives proved rebellions fruits alive and living in us. Opening my heart to desire bigger and more thrilling adventures than childhood allowed. Adventures of walking to stores, library, and school enjoyed a safe and secure environment within a community of similarly held values, as a young adult the bigger the adventure the more the risk and the more severe the consequences, because the environment was like Simba in Lion King. Going into the tempting unknown where who knew what was lurking around the next corner waiting to bring challenges for which I was not prepared.

As far back as I can remember connection with family and friends was important to me. Striving to make connection within gathering times with parents, grandparents, church clubs, and extended family, my hunger for relationship sought satisfaction. Aunt Ruth gave me some of the positive attention I craved; teaching me how to blow bubbles with bubble gum, tie my shoes, create ABC characters with silly attributes and have me for sleep overs with my cousin who was like a big sister to me, including me in her friendships. Living in a small house next to my Mom-mom and Pop-Pop who also showed me love and acceptance; visiting between our homes located a few miles apart offered a place of belonging. Mom-mom made me feel special, as my picture of 1 year in age remained on her dresser until her passing. Never minding when I enjoyably respectfully searched out jewelry treasures, in her bedroom, with the awe and wonder of a little girl hoping someday to have her own beautiful accessories for adornment.Eventually coming to inherit a few pieces which I wear today. One bracelet made around 1912, that I wear often, was a gateway to hear God speak prophetically. The band held a heart shape engraved with two smaller hearts and a flower with five petals. On a Sunday morning in church while worshipping I looked upon it and heard these words; "That big heart is My heart and the two small hearts represent you and Gary and each petal on the flower, one of your five children." Not forgetting His words, each time I wear it, I will always be grateful to my grandmother for the privilege of inheritance and to God for his love which encompasses my family. Mom Mom and Pop Pop were both forthright in their care for me. As a child they had moved to Atlanta for Pop Pop's work, writing me personal letters and post cards. As an adult I discovered Pop Pop rendered a pencil drawing of me inspired by a photograph, the one displayed by Mom-Mom. Material treasures revealing signs of their inner love. Time given specifically to me that met emotional need for loving acceptance.

Pop Pop was never annoyed when I went to his workroom to watch and question his techniques. His success as a pattern maker for children's clothing is knowledge and time, he gave which today is used in my creative processes when working on any sewing. My children enjoyed last minute costumes for school projects done without paper pattern, only my thoughts to guide their creation. Pop Pop's knowledge and antics always made being at their house fun. Whipped cream brought out of the cold refrigerator to fill my mouth with yummy goodness, watermelon seed spitting contests at family picnics, two candy drawers (one his and one ours), and visits to our home sometimes for ice cream on hot sweltering summer evenings. Being younger than most of the grandchildren and having them close helped me find love amidst the storms of life; a welcome interruption of positive relationship. Summer adventures to their cabin in "God's Country", where shooting target, swimming in a spring pond: which was frigid, and tastes of locally crafted ice cream were experiences of goodness that eased my pain of rejection.

Feelings of rejection appeared visiting relatives where there were no girls, but not all Sunday visits were void of girls and good memories. Girls cousins were a welcome reprieve as they offered a side of female perspective I needed. A tom-boy defensiveness was put aside on these occasions giving me emotional connection to my female qualities. Play time was focused on girl activity, dress up, and dolls. In the neighborhood it was mostly boys or tomboys. I had a hard time in that arena connecting to my feminine side. Often looking to boys and men for attention, this out of the ordinary behavior, was left unaddressed by my parents. My exclusion due to lack of female relatives, on my mother's side, who were my age made it necessary to try fitting into the boy's activities which they resented, offering up abuse to keep me away. Retaliating the abuse with physical attacks and anger seemed my only defense. Both positive and negative experiences left imprints for the future. My mind will, and emotions were open to both making the struggle to find acceptance real. Feelings of loneliness and rejection were very familiar: compensated with boldness; a pretense of strength. Keeping up the defense was an ebb and flow, mostly flow, as home and school were the places I spent most of my time, requiring effort in acceptable appearances.

Mother was task oriented in handling her family. Emotional support of correction and guidance were lacking, put onto my father if a big problem. By escalation time, we faced anger not loving correction. The remembrance of only a lone spanking is in my memory bank, for getting snow in my boots on the way home from school. Repeatedly after being told not to do so (mother was tired of cleaning up the wet mess), Father was called upon to administer correction. Getting home across a snow-covered bridge, with mounds of inviting white snow after release from a school desk seemed unavoidable in the first grade. I thought as I grew older, I certainly had done much worse to deserve a spanking. My childlike mind didn't comprehend the difference between childlike play and the work it caused when the snow melted into puddles on the floor. One very abusive incident of correction to my younger brother caused me great angst, leading me to intervene on his behalf, the reality of it stayed years into the future and made me shuddered for what I had observed and tried to understand. What must have been my own parents experience to react with such force? Only God can know and heal these wounds unseen to the eye. Forgiveness and compassion to understand my parents past softened the trauma. These types of traumatic imprints on life must learn to be given to the Lord in prayer, requesting understanding from God's all-knowing perspective. Searching meditation of the scriptures and intimacy with the voice of the Shepherd, will save the soul from the ravages of the past and deliver us into His peace and rest.

As a child my understanding was immature at best and communication of an affirming nature was a spare commodity. Mother kept a clean and tidy home, extending hospitality including deliciously prepared favorite foods: homemade applesauce, vegetable beef soup, and breakfast each morning. She was an excellent cook. Our wardrobes were always neatly laundered, ironed and updated as we grew; with the best that our budget afforded, most often more than that of peers who told me so as an adult that they thought I had the perfect life growing up.

Even though the communication impressed on me conveyed I was difficult and different; leaving me a feeling of insecurity, unassured that I was neither loved nor wanted by my immediate family. Mother was often asked the question "How many children do you have?' repeatedly I heard, "We have three boys and Susan." Demeaned and lesser than a daughter, her words left me feeling more like an "it. Confusion kept me guessing about my identity, showing forth in unseemly precocious behaviors, as I looked for love and affirmation outside my home. I walked through childhood into young womanhood desperate to answer the question "Who am I?"; living my life lead by emotions of the moment I was experiencing, I wanted answers from someone who cared for me and wanted my best interest.

Only three years before, in fear of what people would think of me, instead of breaking an engagement, I walked down the aisle of my childhood church, talking to myself in silence, "Well, if this doesn't work, I can always get a divorce." Who walks down the aisle toward the man you are going to marry thinking these thoughts? I did and they would stay hidden within my soul until years passed and I saw their power for what they reaped in my life. Failure began with an abusive fight on the honeymoon and in retrospect I gave myself permission to failed relationship by giving agreement to divorce even before marriage.

Success is fleeting when foundations are unstable. Both of ours were, from early childhood. Having no idea that they were broken and connected to many dysfunctional relational qualities, we enter fragmented relationships trying to make sense of the picture at hand with only a portion of it. Where are the missing pieces? Our experience of life becomes our normal understanding of how life is lived. I knew I wasn't happy but kept getting emotional highs by living my motto: "I'll try anything once!" Though thrilling, these risks were taking me deeper into darkness of soul. I had no clue how to see past the problems my choices created. Cultural rebellion and revolution of the time offered many opportunities to experiment with ideas before seen as unacceptable societal norms. Changing perspective or fixing attitudes were things I knew nothing about, and they alluded me in even greater measure as my few guiding principles and expectations faded into the background allowing emotionally charged decisions on my path leading to destruction.

Foundations of faith, family, identity, government, nations, and education were toppling established roles of authority and structure. A quote from a narrative on my life written in college by my daughter, sums it up well.

"Everyone was trying to determine what was appropriate and break the mold of past generations. The idea of finding oneself at all cost seemed to be a very real experience for a lot of youth." -Hannah C. Barr

Those were the years of experimenting with drugs, sexuality, education; pushing boundaries that had stood in our nation since its inception. Coupled with the influence of cultural changes and adding to revolutionary transformation were individual experiences, one of which for me reinforced my questions of self-worth.

It happened Thanksgiving weekend the year I turned eight. Father and mother opened the door of hospitality for my brother's fiancée and a friend from military school to join our family celebration. On the night following our celebration dinner, it was agreed that the friend would watch me and my younger brother, while the others would go out to dinner. Watching television, after getting into pj's and later sending my brother off to sleep, the friend moved over to sit beside me on the sofa. He questioned me, "Do you like to snuggle with your dad?" Of course, "Yes" upon which the questioning continued after he moved in closer. "Does your Daddy touch you like this?" His moves became intrusive and leading and there was no where to escape an eighteen-year-old, stronger and more imposing, he was not taking any chances to not satisfy his evil lustful desires. Fear gave way, his horrible actions violated my youth and innocence. Looking for justice and protection, the opportunity arose the next evening when alone with one of my parents to recount actions the evening before, the response was anything but just and protective. "You shouldn't let boys touch you that way". My soul confused and negated of hope for supportive compassion, was disheartened. Blaming myself affected my life for many years, even decades. Subconsciously, ruining many relationships and Thanksgiving Holidays. My other parent was not told of this occurrence and forty-eight years later opportunity to reveal the molestation came to pass. No way of knowing it had been kept from them, they voiced the sorrow I had longed to hear all those years. Freedom to release my hurt, and receive a long-awaited apology for this act, brought me one step closer to freedom in my soul and identity. It had been a search I started in childhood.

My desire for freedom began in fourth grade when I read "The Freedom Train" on the life of Harriet Tubman. She was a slave in the South who longed to be free and chose to do something about it. Her courage and bravery, mounted her flight, helping many to also fulfill their longing to be free from the oppression of slavery as well. Freedom to live by free will choices, not bound by the will of those who would keep them subdued with fear to break their spirit. Stolen by molestation and enforced by acts of unkind abusive relationships, innate senses were warped and twisted, driving me to harmful behavior which was the only sense of life I ever knew. The plum line was crooked, the way undefined and undisciplined and felt anything but free. I lived in a free country but what did it mean to live free?

Our United States Constitution is the foundation of freedom laid out to give our country and people the identity of equality for all. We are all created with certain and unalienable rights. What are they and how do we gain understanding and knowledge of them? Harriet's plight changed me causing me to become aware of others struggles. Circumstances in our lives were different, I was not a slave to a plantation owner, but I was a slave to man. To my own being and to the desire to please to the point of sacrificing my being in ungodly behaviors. My definition of freedom began to form with a desire to help myself and others make free will choices and deciding to treat others the way I wanted myself to be treated. Minimal in the scope of my life, but still a child, I realized all people were important; to be treated equally by being given freedom of will within parameters set by God.

Harriet's story and this new knowledge motivated me to stand for equality of being in people. At age ten, my eyes were opened to see bigotry and racism even within my own heritage and boldly proclaimed its injustice and equality as I saw it manifesting. I had found strength to speak; although mostly within the family. In school noticing abuse aroused compassion for others not given respect, greeting not ignoring them, defending them in conversation. At home my defense of those not accepted would be reprimanded as disrespect of elders, but justice and compassion required retort with respect for all, stating "Everyone's blood is the same color and we are all created by God."

Only after making a commitment to Christ did he make me aware of the foundation laid then that would shape my ministry now. He would use it to build intercession in my future and ministry to many who were also in need of freedom. Not only physical freedom but also emotional, thoughtful, and spiritual freedom. However, that said, all freedoms without spiritual freedom remain out of reach. Jesus openly proclaimed that He is the way, the truth and the life and no man can come to the Father except through Him. John 14:6. We must know our Father and willingly choose to love Him through Christ, and therefore all whom he created. My personal path to freedom was long but none the less continually leading to wholeness. The challenges of relationship and the counter desire to succeed pushed me ever forward to new uncharted territory relationally.

Counseling for my failing marriage circumstantially set my journey to freedom on a new course; 1979-1980 shifted momentum from the direction of self being controlled by emotion to recognizing why and how choices could be made more thoughtfully with understanding of consequence. Growth was not an easy task. My counselor and I worked six months together before I could apply consistently the principles learned in our sessions. An outside perspective challenging my comfort zones required I learn to trust the process of growth toward new ways of relationship. Seeing the benefits of constructive analysis to peace and most destructive continual defense of my person who was afraid of looking inwardly. Facing myself in an unfamiliar perspective given to me by someone who actually had good intentions to help me was new territory. A new prototype for all future relationships. To this day I continue to love the challenges presented for growth toward healthy relationship.

Prior to this shift in 1978, my husband and I accepted guardianship of his eleven-year-old brother, left in need when his mother only 48 years old passed into eternity. She had been deeply wounded by unfaithfulness leading to divorce only one year prior to her death. Her heart wounded and broken as her husband would return only to leave again many times over. I could see beyond her behavior, into the pain behind her eyes and was motivated to love her. Attempts to drown the pain in alcohol had taken her to bad health at a very young age. Her woundedness was obvious in her words. Spilling out each conversation in hurt, tears and lack of fulfillment. Love for people found me reaching out, easing troubles through care, trying to in some way make her feel loved and not a failure. By meeting needs I sensed would bring healing and healthy affection, our relationship, five years in the making, was mutual in love and respect. We found joy, and solace in our relationship. But the damages were extensive, and I alone was not enough. She died never reaching her potential.

After her death, a one-bedroom apartment would not suffice for our growing family and my generous father, most likely moved by his own loss at the same age, helped us secure a relatively new house on an acre wooded lot in the same township of my own childhood years. Still my home to this day, it stands along a road in the Appalachian Mountains; a dirt road in the past, leading to my horse's home in a neighboring hamlet. At twelve years of age the stories of my father's farm horse and visits to relatives still caring for their own horses were key to my growing desire to own a horse. At age eleven, pestering my father to fulfill my want, he challenged me to work for half of the purchase price. He told me if accomplished he would match my hard -earned funds. Challenge accepted!

Earlier at age nine, encouraged by Daddy to enjoy trail rides at a near-by stable, the sounds, smells and touch of these large gracious and strong animals had a warmth and energy inviting me to pleasure with loving big eyes and soft muzzles to adventuring joy awaiting atop their back with gentle rocking motion set to scenic panoramas not available from the ground. Riding had the sense of freedom, the exhilaration of just me and the horse on an adventure and most of the time freedom from difficulties of life.

Setting out, highly motivated to complete my challenge, I worked various jobs such as babysitting, mowing, and door to door sales of Christmas cards. Mom Mom (Mom's mother) had passed her sales on to me to help. After only a year, extatically reaching my goal; I became familiar with the dirt road that would eventually become my path to home. On a designated day Daddy would drive me in anticipation over that mountain road to the stable of a high school chum, Art, who had a bay gelding for sale. He was a fair-sized American Saddlebred, 12 years old, like me and stood 15.3 hands tall; retired from life as an Amish buggy horse, due to skittish behavior. His name was Phares (pronounced "Ferris"), which means, not unlike my own name, beautiful, fair and handsome.

Unfamiliar with English dressage, and only having experience with western neck reigning, after a quick time of instruction, I mounted for our first adventure together as horse and rider. Pulling him right to walk a short distance to the longer path along the paddock; the second turn had already given Phares an idea of my English inexperience and my unfamiliarity with him. Knowingly he was in control, immediately carrying me to full girth speed along the entire fence line, past and through tree branches, shaking any confidence I may have acquired previously. Full speed ahead, rounding the final turn to our starting point, I landed; humbled and fearful atop his neck in cartoonish fashion. Round 1: Phares 1- Me 0!

Quaking in by boots, literally, I was met by the voice of experience. Father's words of wisdom were not what I wanted to hear but what I needed to hear if I was ever to succeed at controlling Phares. I now realize this is the key to success in life as well. Hearing our Heavenly Father speak what we need not what we want to hear, guarantees a successful path on our journey of life. It would have been easy to give up at that point, throwing my dreams to the wind, but father spoke authoritatively that I needed to get back up on that horse; not letting my fear overcome my desire to have a horse and carrying the lesson learned into my future where I would face more abuse that would try to keep me from my destiny in Christ. Fear effecting my soul would rule me into adulthood but the seed my father planted would eventually make me a warrior against fear and its debilitating effects. That lesson prepared me for obedience to my Heavenly Father who by His ways and Spirit would help me to overcoming victory.

The house on the dirt road, now paved, is the way to home where I would begin a new path toward maturity. Feeling up to the task of caring for my brother-in-law, girded by my years of childcare and an established relationship of five years along with love and respect for one another; offered him encouragement and security to begin his new path as well. Other options for his new journey seemed lacking; the familiar setting of the only child, requiring adjustment to other children. Times of change including new school and his now absent mother would be difficult enough. Children had always been a haven for me, returning affection without fear of rejection. Our community of young families gave plenty of afterschool opportunity to help moms with associated care which yielded priceless experience for what I now faced and an acceptance for which my soul longed. Now years later, I had no fear of raising a child at a very young age and beginning my parenting in our new home.

Settling into the house after looking at other options. Dad, again using his own wisdom, preferred the newness of this one as compared to the older character details I preferred in some of the others. He figured we had enough responsibility to handle without the additional possibility of repairs and remodeling. The newer home however did have qualities both positive and negative that would affect my life. We still enjoy campfires in the original pit built the weekend we moved. I wish I had kept count of the number of fires enjoyed over the years, they were many and often spurring fellowship, evangelism and teaching in later years. God spoke to me through the scriptures of being a modern-day High Priest of the fellowship fires. Through the years our home invited many nations and peoples to hospitality around those fires offering fellowship to Christ's family and those who would like to know more about His family.

However, negatively the house's seventies décor was dark, encompassing dark walnut woods for cabinets and paneling and multi-colored dark semi-shag carpets. Lack of sunlight from over shadowing woodland, combined with décor in dark colors wreaked havoc with my emotional state. Triggering an awareness of depression, I didn't like. I would do all I could to overcome it's crippling effects and educating myself with design classes would overcome darkness of house and continual study of the Bible my soul.

New responsibilities of guardianship, a bigger home, my full-time position in my father's pizza manufacturing business and part-time college studies were a lot to juggle. Just prior to all these changes I had agreed to fill in as temporary truck driver laying aside my administrative assistant, to my father, position. Loading, driving and delivery were a relief from the mental exhaustion of paperwork, emotional stress as well and provided physical strengthening with freedom away from co-workers who saw me as the spoiled daughter, a thorn in the side. Again, I was breaking through socially accepted roles of the past for women's freedom taking on a traditionally held male job. Mother was horrified I was traveling at night. Sometimes many hours into surrounding states as far north as Albany, New York and south into Maryland and east to New Jersey, father assured her I could handle the responsibility and duration of only four months. I enjoyed traveling; sitting in my big Mercedes box truck above the traffic, loading and unloading trucks brought physical strength I had not known before. I reveled in new adventurous freedom, tackling experiences that helped me reach deeper into myself for strength to succeed.

The end of June 1978, I took a large delivery to our warehouse in Allentown. During unloading I became nauseous and dizzy, blaming it on lack of food and physical exertion, it would not be a long time until a test would reveal a baby to be born early the following year. Emotions ran the gamut from happy to worry.

Quickly I ceased from my habits of cigarettes and drinking alcohol, I wanted to do what was best for the child within. Reality was giving me a lot of responsibility and I was not at all confident in my ability to handle it.

Our party lifestyle was no longer an option. My rocky marriage, emotional highs and lows, took me on a roller coaster ride of hills, up and down, no end in sight and no peace to accompany me. Any relationship with authority of any magnitude or weight was mostly non-existent, since after high school I had decided to do as I pleased, starting with the decision to openly smoke in my parents' home like the rest of family and guests. The habit developed after age eleven when smoking with friends at a neighbor's tree house. Gathering supply of cigarettes from our parents, we tested the "waters". Not even Eva, running toward us, her deep baritone voice yelling as she saw the smoke seeping through the floor and walls, thwarted our continuance of this habit. By eighteen I had a full-blown addiction nurtured by rebellion and addiction. I started drinking at age fifteen at home when I was offered wine with dinner. Until age 18, it was alcohol fueling my wild behavior. Then it was combined with pot and other occasional drugs. Drugs was one vice I thought I wanted nothing to do with until a very good friend confessed, she was experimenting. I respected her judgement as she always seemed to have made good choices. It was the hook the devil used to take me further into his realm of darkness. And I swallowed it hook, line and sinker.

As for association with church, I had been required to attend up through graduation of high school and now only attended on Easter and Christmas holidays. The only authority presently was my discipline for studies and my father's question as to my engagement choice. Certainly, it should have been questioned. Only I was deceived to think my choice was exclusive of anyone else and the consequences seemingly insignificant compared to the moments of celebration with friends, also choosing the same. Current decisions had a feeling of unity, my friends and culture shared in my rebellion and experimental attitudes, and our enemy the devil will make sure you have every opportunity to revel in his vices.

Convincing myself to believe that every action inconsistent with the values of my parents was easy. We all think we're right until we're proven wrong. The fact that their experience had taught them lessons and gave them concern for my future wellbeing and provision held no sway against the longing to be acceptable in the eyes of my peers. My intended spouse was steeped in the current youth culture of substance abuse which halted his education at age 15, willfully choosing to leave high school. Never mind facts. I was accustomed to a whole different lifestyle; having a new wardrobe every season, vacationing yearly, fine dining on occasion, including every need provided for by my parents. Provisions were expected and forthcoming. In the background, the chasm of differences ignored. I thought human love could bridge the gap between us. Hope of influencing him through increased cultural and family experience became lost hope when I realized he didn't care about growth, and my expectation of provision wrongly pushed me forward on the path of continuing parental funding to fill the gap of what we could not afford with our combined income. I didn't know how to adjust to the lack of flow, the decision making. My emotions were in control and no matter who it was I was relating too; they took the forefront in the decision-making process. Husband, family, friends, acquaintances, all were subject to the moods of my emotion and vice versa about making decisions on the swing of the cultural pendulum.

We were watching one couple after another marry and within a few years ditch their marriages. Our circle of friends included a couple who was ten years older and married with four children. By all appearances, they seemed solid and had a working marriage relationship. But one day on the job, the husband suggested that an extramarital affair would bring emotional satisfaction to my frustrations of an emotionally and physically missing spouse. At that point I was a hold out on cheating because I had always viewed marriage correctly in the sense of monogamy. I did not think I wanted to go beyond that boundary, I was about to find out susceptibility to the wiles of the enemy. One by one, allowing him to destroy my other previously held values through desire to please myself. This one was no exception. He already had strongholds of which I knew nothing about.

Only a couple of months passed, arrangements were made for me to enjoy a weekend away at this couple's mountain retreat with a group of women. Unaware of plans made to entice me into extra-marital relationship, the weekend revealed a subtle and slippery slope to join in this groups consenting unfaithfulness to their spouses.

The first night out on that weekend, the girls had set up a scenario with their partners. I believe two of us were a part of the plan. A marijuana high and "friends" manipulative words set the scene, "Hey, you need a dancing partner. A handsome guy over there is looking your way." "When I wink at you that means he is looking." Trying to ignore and laugh it off, an arm soon crossed my shoulder. I didn't see him coming. "Would you like to dance?" That dance led to a year affair, ended by mutual agreement that divorcing and remarrying each other would never be the right choice. Truly appreciating one another, I realized for maybe the first time in my life I could be a different woman and feel loved by a man, but that was not enough.

In the end I had left behind a small part of my self-hatred and replaced it with confidence that it was possible to find love and acceptance. God would lead me to seek forgiveness in a written apology to his wife, after my own salvation was established in Christ. My last meeting with him expressed my care and concern for his own salvation and my hope that someday under God's plan we would see each other in heaven. God would lead me to cut off all ties, emotionally, and spiritually so I would eventually be able to learn the path to freedom for myself and others.

Continuing my search for acceptance, college course work in business administration was my hope for a dream to become the president of my father's company, another step to be recognized in traditional male position. If my dream were achieved, my acceptance by my father would be a partial fulfillment of my personhood. I believed it would show him I was a capable young woman worthy of his respect. My perception was warped, Daddy had his own ideas about women and especially his daughter. He loved me but certainly never had the idea that I could fill the role of president of his company. That was reserved for someone else. His idea of a woman was my mother. My idea of a woman was all of that and more, eventually seeking to become a Proverbs 31 woman.

Education and counseling advanced my thinking toward understanding the results of my choices. Learning from my beloved counselor, my faulty choices based in emotions instead of reasoning changed the amount of peace in my circumstances, paving the new avenue toward my freedom as a being. But of course, this was still not enough to make me feel what I knew innately, that I was made to be someone with purpose, someone valued, loved and accepted. Inklings and rays of hope and light were showing up to move me forward in my search. I shared with my counselor my newfound faith in Christ and was mocked with sarcastic words, "Of course, you have." He did not deter me. The tools I received from his own hand had chipped away hardened parts of my soul but not all. My strong will wanted to find complete satisfaction for the longings in my heart.

Now, many years of seeking faith in Christ, study of the bible, practicing His teachings, elder believer's input, and introspection in relationship has taught me the path to freedom is trusting God's word as the point of departure for all wisdom, knowledge and understanding. Opening my heart to the pain of growth, no matter the cost, was the only way to experience life in the full. That fullness is a process. A cup gets filled one drop at a time, a rose grows one season into another and the blossoms, year after year, dying in between seasons to regain strength and increased beauty for the next season. So is our journey of seasons through life. My pregnancy was another season to bring me more of God's goodness and fulfillment.

A beautiful son was born on a clear crisp winter day in February, followed by unseasonable warmth. The weeks following allowed time outside in the sun. As most first-time moms; scared to death of the possibility of birth, after 14 hours and declarations of "I want to quit!", my joy was enlarged and my love as well. Being a mom felt good, the fear I felt of new motherhood dissipated and passed with birthing. Holding and nurturing my child was enjoyable. Newness of life was refreshing, and the challenges of motherhood embraced. My marriage encompassed by new life in our child and love for him surmounted the marital struggles of the past months. An amount of revival came in the excitement of joy. I really wanted now to work on family life. To lay aside the past and move hopeful into the reality of a happy family, working together to make a home. The euphoria was short lived, very soon my anger at lack of care and selfishness that left me alone every night with a colicky child, was more than I could handle. At twenty-three, I would begin to see my brokenness when circumstances stirred me to awaken to much needed change. Deeply disturbed one night by my six-month son's nonstop crying, I was alone with no one to relieve me to help in his care; I felt helpless to calm him. Anger rose up. My husband's abandonment, most every night, to partying was not the family life envisioned, although looking back my own example lived, was that of a mother who took on mostly all house and childcare. Like a wave overtaking me with its sudden overwhelming rage, I found myself shaking my son, yelling for him to be quiet. Awakened by feelings of horror, reality rising within my soul, frightened of my being; and struck through with awareness of the abuse just inflicted on the son I love. Aware of a deadly capability to do irreparable harm: something I had not experienced prior. Only moments passed thrusting me immediately toward life changing decisions. Quickly before my anger could overtake me in its grip, I decided to end my marriage.

Thinking separation would alleviate the source of anger was my motive. Little did I realize my anger had rooted at three months of age from another traumatic event which would only be revealed to me over 25 years later.

My six-month-old son's relentless crying triggered anger to surface in an unthinkable explosion, shaking his little body, victimized unknowingly because of wrongly directed emotion.

This act of rage lead to my separation; to the engagement of a counselor, at the insistence of my mortified parents. We were some of the first to be caught in the initial wave of increased broken marriages of our generation. We all attended the first counseling session together for an outside opinion of the circumstances and hopefully emerge with a plan to heal. Moving into action in our first session, it was decided that counsel as a couple once a week was needful. Three weeks passed, anxious but hopeful, I liked being in a safe place able to express my viewpoint. However, that week, when posed the question of continued growth and desire, hope for reconciliation was dashed when my husband expressed "I like who I am, and I don't need to change." He did not wish to continue. On the other side, my desire was to continue toward a healthier life exploring the possibilities for future stability. My closed persona took three months to open to my counselor about more then the weather and current circumstances. His perceptions included a diagnosis that I thought like and man and made decisions based on my emotions were areas of work. He wanted to dig up fallow ground allowing the real free me to emerge. After six months and progress toward a model of healthy communication, I would be advised to extend myself to vulnerability within a group of twelve meeting weekly, in addition to individual sessions

as needed. Group therapy was meant to expand experience
to trusting and being trusted by others beyond the safety and
protection of our counselor. Principles learned could then be
applied to any relationship.

During the next twelve weeks I would develop and learn new
relational skills through psychodrama; a very carefully guided
experience of traumatic past events re-enacted by the group. One
of those was with a woman who had lost her daughter to a sudden
death. Lack of understanding and acceptance caused her to have
manic depression bouts that totally immobilized her day to day
function. Sitting, side by side, the first night, she clutched her
handbag tightly to her lap, looking ready to escape in a moment.
Each was given a chance to express why we had decided to explore
the group, stating our hopes for impact. Hers was a story that
stirred my compassion. Added to that, she said I reminded her of
her deceased daughter, causing me strange feelings. Upon our exit
of the session and entrance to the elevator, my heart and thoughts
turned to hope of helping her resolve her grief. I lifted a prayer of
sorts with that request.

Not many weeks passed, and each had a chosen client's name
on it by virtue of the counselor's wisdom of timing. About the
third week, Anna, the women who had lost her daughter was
chosen. Re-enacting and re-arranging circumstances surrounding
her lack of closure allowed vocalization of words she wanted to say
but hadn't been able. Her daughter had stayed at college to study
her nursing, while others went home to enjoy a long weekend
away from the cares of study. Four days would pass before she was
found, lying lifeless on her dorm floor. The time allowed the body
to decompose beyond recognition, disallowing a normal viewing

of the body. Anna needed closure. Becoming the stand-in daughter for her drama, the prayer I prayed was answered. Most amazingly, as I relayed the events to my own mother, she recognized the facts to be the real life of her new friend from a nursing refresher course just completed. What? I knew something seemed to be at work here beyond what I perceived. Sadly, that was Anna's last night with the group but not our last encounter. Eventually, I would visit with my mother at Anna's home and my mother's friendship would last many years until Anna passed, having struggled every year on anniversaries with ugly depression.

Culmination of the group was a marathon of sessions set in the beautiful countryside of Doc's farmhouse; sharing meals, rooms and unexplored dramas for those of us yet to face our individual group work. Knowing my turn was coming, fear of stepping into the circle of familiar friendly faces kept my mind wondering, I anxiously anticipated the arrival of my own drama. Wearing down our defenses by physical exhaustion with an extremely late-night Friday and early awakening Saturday, we would fit two dramas into the morning and await announcement of whose time would come after lunch. Each session brought similar emotional stories of hurt, pain and woundedness, to which the group responded empathetically with support and encouragement. I supposed that if others survived the vulnerability, I would as well.

Doc started out the drama accompanying each one as together they walked around the large comfortable environs of his family gathering room now turned womb for the unfolding birth of embedded emotions of past events. Continual questions with forethought probed to uncover what was hidden. Poking memories evoked thoughts and emotions to break down walls of

self-protection that kept me prisoner to their anger, preventing
the real me from being. Increasing greatly in intensity and
pressure he questioned repeatedly "Why do you hate men? Do
you remember events that would have caused these emotions?"
"How do you feel about certain persons?"; these just a few of
the questions that stirred inner rage to fast and furious paces.
With great determination and strength of emotional momentum
causing Doc's legs to exhaust, he couldn't keep up. Increasing
intensity of unrelenting focused motion like a train speeding to
destiny; duration three hours. Eventually succumbing as well,
exhaustion accompanied sobbing tears in upheaval of my soul's
lifetime of suppression. The answers to his questions remained
hidden, cloaked in anger. Collapsing to the floor, arms of empathy
surrounded me; these had also known pain and willingly shared
to bring healing. How was I to feel about hurts imbedded so
deeply my soul? Only anger, not specific cause for my resented
identity of woman was released. No catharsis. Strong resistance
was not allowing me freedom to speak. Walls of self-protection
were high and thick. After break-neck pace, words of empathy and
embracing hugs were affirming progress made toward freedom.
I had no idea how the unraveling and cleansing of the effects
of anger and its cohorts would continue for many years, until
allowing blossom of my being into beautiful freedom of soul: my
original intended destiny. Like a shaken bottle of carbonation,
opening to release a small amount of the pent-up unresolved
conflict, the path of emotional damages; deep ruts surrounded by
broken walls, needed rebuilt under the direction of newly acquired
tools of restoration. The bottle of emotions had been shaken
and would now be unable to stay contained because someone

cared enough to risk the shaking to uncork the ugly; looking for something good inside of me. That day was possibly my first experience of going beyond reality in a group setting into the waiting arms of love, comfort and understanding; a freedom that felt safe. Although more digging was required.

Counseling afforded the opportunity to study anonymously under my therapist, an adjunct professor at my college, who advised taking his course on Thanatology (death and dying). Opening foundational destruction and rebuilding necessary for stability by virtue of content. God was encouraging self -examination with agitation to change. Combined circumstances truly had me asking "What do I believe?" Sharing varied and somewhat strange and unfamiliar beliefs, fellow students ranged from traditional, to extremes; like death as the finality of days, making up one's own reality of a death and non-Christian religious beliefs of which I knew little. Necessity churned the information to form questions.

What did I believe? Certainly, I believed in a Creator God... but was unsure of any relativity to my own life choices. He was distant. Not tangible. Times growing up, I felt a connection and desire to love Him, but limited searching impeded my experiential knowledge and was not something I had yet explored as an adult. Until age of eighteen, when my parents ended required church attendance. Attending as faithfully as my parents on a weekly basis; I was involved in choir, youth group, making confirmation at fifteen, studying included three years of catechism exploring Father, Son and Holy Spirit ending with confirmation. During these years desire heightened but soon waned under the social activities put as high priority. Politically charged sermons, requiring written personal assessment, posed questions of relativity to church. The pastor offended by my inquisitive thoughts, voiced angrily that I should find a new church if I didn't like the sermons. His response did not fit my perception of the Christian teaching I had learned in the past three years. The definition of catechism: instruct someone in the principles of Christian religion by means of question and answer. His response left me confused about what little faith, if any, I had and surely founded distrust of pastoral care. However, any rebuttal of making a commitment would not be tolerated and I would make confirmation with unanswered questions and only the commitment to do as I was told. At home, mealtime prayer of repetition was the extent of family spiritual involvement, and bible reading, only what was read in church. Church was the limitation of my spiritual knowledge and during a session of World Cultures expounding on the history of Christianity our teacher asked a question about being Christian to which I answered, "I go to church". Sharply he replied, "Going to church does not make you Christian!" Another public, peer viewed, humiliation left me wondering and retreating away from any form of Christianity I knew and deeper into following emotions. Except for a couple strange occurrences like being frequently awakened by a "tickling" demon which disturbed my sleep, spiritual experiences evaded me. Running to my dad provided protective sense, when another realistic spiritual experience happened at seventeen, a senior in high school. "The Exorcist" came out in theatres. Normally, not attuned to scary genre, but invited by a childhood friend on a date, we drove quite a distance to view it on the big screen. Hearing the basis of the plot was true story motivated my choice to overcome fear of the scary. Only twenty minutes into it, emotionally uncomfortable with the thought of its reality, I could watch no longer. Excusing myself with apology to my date, the lobby offered a haven to wait the duration alone. Those twenty minutes of perceived true story disrupted my sleep or lack thereof for four nights. Seeking the protection of father, it was the one night he opened the scriptures to me, leading me to the 23rd Psalm with instruction to continue reading until my fears were quieted. My heart was sensitive however immature. Coming to understand spiritual activity was yet to be. However, I was gaining experiences that would be valuable once I learned to view them as such.

Middle school had previously presented many challenges to my character. One via a fellow church member, also a teacher, who judged cheering tryouts. Cheering since the fourth grade, developed a love for the outdoor sport, where shouting loud for all to hear encouraged our team, "The Saints", to victory. "Once a cheerleader always a cheerleader" I say. Encouragement does not lie dormant if it is part of who you are in your spirit. My "team" name has remained the same. Loud, energetic and determined to succeed, I would achieve the highest scores of all the candidates. However, this judge determined to hold the standard of character for role model as a cheerleader to a higher place then my character could reach. Because of her sway, I was held back to a substitute position on the team. Angry and hateful words toward her, outside of the tryouts, this teacher would determine that in order to succeed, changing my bad reputation going forward to next year would establish eligibility for full-time position. The hurt, used for introspection, caused me to recognize the need to clean up my act and the teacher's judgment ultimately helped. I made the team the following year and was selected that year for other role model positions on student council, the court of our King and Queen of Hearts Dance and Honor Society. It felt good to achieve accomplishments through better choices.

Relationally I had always, even from a very young age, been attracted to the opposite gender. Using feminine shenanigans, to attract and gain affections, became normal pattern. Promiscuity invaded social settings, pushing socially accepted boundaries to find acceptance was at its heart. My identity was wrapped up in giving myself away for momentary acceptance. All my social activities placed opportunity to do so at my fingertips so to speak.

Mother enrolled lots of activity to fill my days and evenings. Brownies, Girl Scouts, Cheering, Choir, 4-H Club, sewing, party planning, church camp, swimming, horseback riding, shopping, sleepovers, school sporting events; all these and more kept me learning many skills, good and bad, expanding my opportunity to find unsupervised time for trouble. What they did not give me was familial connection.

Supervising these activities were adults who fell on both sides of the continuum in a wide array of good to bad influence. One from Girl Scouts took the opportunity to further damage my identity calling me "queer" when I had removed a top layer of sleepwear. Remaining covered, the heat from the fireplace on the top bunk next to it was making me extremely hot and sweaty. Her loud and again public humiliation was heard by the entire troop recorded in their mind, effecting their view of me as I perceived. At least my mind was effected for sure. The effect moved me toward experimentation with gender orientation and united with my already faulty views of self, I went further down the path of confusion and hate for myself, though ultimately looking for the real me.

This type of public humiliation began in kindergarten when it was announced by nonother than my "best friend", to my entire class that I had had an accident, calling one and all "come and see", reinforced by the teacher who displayed a portion of the accident result in full-view of the class. Second grade brought another total humiliation, my out of line chatting was called out and disciplined by placing tape across my mouth and putting me under a table in the back of the room for an extended time; laughed and mocked with sneers by classmates, those feelings were not quickly dismissed. At home my siblings added to self-hatred excluding me and acting toward me with hurtful words and actions of hostility. One year my Christmas present was non other than collected toe-nail clippings and belly button fuzz. A gift supposed to be a joke, only served to tell me that I was not worth a real gift. Laughter and no correction or apology added on top were fodder for hate.

Self-hatred was beginning to take out what little I liked about myself. Feeling a lack of self-worth would become a struggle I would contend with consistently until I came to realize I was valued by God. It wasn't a total wash as some teachers saw good in me; acknowledging leadership qualities imprinted by my father. Socially prominent in business and community, father was a forerunner, developing in 1959 one of the first frozen pizzas on the market in Pennsylvania. Company growth encompassing a five-state area involved our innovative school lunch program using Government Commodities of flour and cheese by voucher to create a rectangle pizza slice that met nutritional standards for a product that could be served to students. Increasing efforts toward expansion allowed for a new state of the art facility to be built in 1970, along with a second production plant in Allentown, PA. The mid-seventies brought all production back to Hershey and another production plant purchased near-by to manufacture a new Pastroli brand which has today become manufactured and named by another company as the Hot Pocket. Under my father's leadership the role model he provided equaled more skills learned. By the mid-eighties, business growth required transition to accommodate increased sales and production.

Of course, its success influenced me at every level of life, beginning with my involvement at inception due to proximity of production which began in our pantry connected to our home. Family and close neighbors were the first producers of the pizzas and I was an interested observer at age 3. With each move of production, my father included me somehow. My belief in his product and skills lead me to respect for him. My father had determined by the grace of God and good stewardship that his path would not be the one he had known during his growing up years and the lack he felt then would not be felt, if he could prevent it, by his wife and children. As his income grew, so did the provision to his children. We never wanted for anything material.

Father and mother were both fashion conscious and started our school year with allowing us to choose new wardrobes. As the years passed, twice a year, new clothes were purchased starting out as mail order from the Sears and Roebuck catalog. Shopping became my mother's and my regular Saturday activity. Becoming accustomed to new outfits for every occasion, by the sixth grade, shopping by myself at a local teen shop, charging it all to my parents account, made my wardrobe envious and a habit that would one day be hard to separate my emotions from when my finances could no longer support it. I began to feel power in dressing through using clothes to present the me I wanted to portray. I didn't know the spiritual implication of promiscuous, seductive dress, but knew it could get attention I badly craved. My family wasn't giving it, so I figured out how to get it my own way.

From all outside appearances our family still seemed well put together years into my life. Friends would tell me so. But I never revealed the rejection, hurt and pain because in our family; we just didn't talk about emotions. Mother, hiding her childhood life in a mountain of homemaking; making breakfast on school days, cleaning, canning, laundry and ironing, preparing cooked meals on an allotted budget, hospitality and the duties of a successful man's wife. She required no regular chores of her children. I recall only helping a few times with clearing the table and dishes. One incident told me my mother's negative feelings toward my Grandmother and in the next breath told me I was just like her. Oh, that hurt of rejection. At nine, training me to iron was her way of trying to keep my huge amount of clothes from adding to ever increasing laundering requirements. One attempt to get my brother and me to clean our stuff up was a barrel placed at the bottom of the basement staircase. Things left to lay, would be thrown into the barrel for us to retrieve, no time allotment, just if we felt the need for whatever was in there. We never felt the need, so the barrel overflowed, and that disciplinary action failed due over accumulation of stuff. Traditional homemaker status pleased my father, allowing his focus role as provider, fulfillment. I think Mom did a fantastic job but lacked fulfillment as a person in her rote daily living. She did enjoy hospitality and accolades came with each occasion but she seemed never to receive them graciously, almost always denying her talents. Her relationships with other women were at church, and business connections, along with neighbors, but the depth was not an emotional vulnerable connection. Our relationship was the same level for many years and never did achieve the depth of intimacy I desired, but we did have affection and make progress toward real communication. I often thought she rather keep her secrets buried and hide her pain with vices. I take some responsibility as my anger often got the best of our communication even into adulthood, but we found our way to reconciliation and appreciation for one another.

As for relationships with my brothers, the two older ones saw me mostly as an object of torment and bother, giving them opportunity for verbal and physical abuse. Torment of my elder brothers was unmet with parental interference until father was around. However, due to his many commitments that was rare on weekdays. My youngest brother with whom I had connection was truly relational, a playmate and friend. Until middle school our after-school playtime involved neighborhood games and comradery. My tomboy attitude helped me to survive a mostly male dominated group of friends.. Saturdays and Sundays, when Daddy was home, I enjoyed learning by watching, or hanging out with him doing whatever his day included. Our similar personalities made fertile soil for planting seeds that assimilated the culture dictating changes in women's roles. Knowledge I gained from our times together was useful in the future. Dad was a risk taker: surveying and adventuring into new territories with business but very protected emotionally as well. Entering young womanhood, the emotional distance with dad was filled with searching out fulfillment in my own daring behavior. His absence emotionally and physically left a void after the age of 14. My life motto supported risks: "I'll try anything once.". Developing within my soul was deep sense of no consequence, emotionally or spiritually, driving me in cycles of self-abuse, using others for personal gain. I thought this was normal since my relational skills were limited to acting out of my emotion.

"Normal" led me down a path that would build protective walls that kept me from seeing correctly. Male relationships were many and varied. Friends and boyfriends. I always seemed to get along with guys better. The attention from father and younger brother made it comfortable and familiar, because up to that point it was women who had humiliated me. Manipulating circumstances achieved the emotional fix I was looking for that I missed at home, but the attention never satisfied the longing and the search went on in vain. I hurt a lot of people this way, not realizing how much until Christ showed me. Asking Him the specifics made the way to freedom from guilt and some things had to be confessed face to face. But prior to realizing, in 1980 my path lead to a very destructive relationship, landing my head into a wall, after being able to see the relationship for what it was in truth. It wasn't the happy, peaceful, one I had hoped for and I chose to end it, thankfully with no lasting injury. The idiom, the straw that broke the camel's back applies. More than the wall and my head needed to be fixed: but how? Where were the answers to a life of peace? ***I figured there had to be more to life than this!*** Crying out in pain and desperation I wanted answers.

On a night a few weeks past the end of that relationship, searching the radio dial at 10 pm, my attention was captured by the mention of God. Halting my search for music and stopping the dial on that station. A man describing a relationship with God that was personal; Jesus had come to earth as a human with the intent of saving us from sin and forgiving us through the sacrifice of his own life on the cross. All of this I had heard in church confession of the Apostle's Creed but I had not heard that I needed to invite Him into my heart where He would dwell eternally by His Holy Spirit who would make me born again into a new life and personal relationship with Him. Personal and new: the key words that sparked my interest. Lutheranism practiced infant baptism and taught only Catechism and commitment to the Lutheran Way would lead to heaven. Luther himself, was a believer and not near as vague as teaching I received. I could not agree that an infant could follow the command of Christ to "Repent and be baptized." **Repentance is the choice of an accountable knowledgeable personal response to God for the forgiveness he offers and the personal relationship He desires. Changing our mind about the way we have lived and choosing "not my will but thy will be done" as the Lord Jesus lived by example.**

CHAPTER 2

The Seed of Love

"When the seed of love is ready to bloom, you will be loved in
return." And a strange new courage entered her. She suddenly
stepped forward, bared her heart, and said 'Please plant the
seed here in my heart."

Much Afraid, Hinds Feet on High Places

Yes, suddenly! Suddenly October of 1980, I was hearing
the answer to my questions, surely my search was headed in a
new direction. Certain my answer to the question posed in the
program's invitation for salvation and new life in Christ was a
definitive "Yes". Jesus would lead me into real relationship offering
true love, forgiveness and freedom. All free for the asking. He had
paid the price for my ransom.

Listening to the end, I walked the hallway to my bedroom,
kneeling in childlike attitude as I had done when I was young, I
confessed my need for what He offered and accepted His invitation
to take up my heart as His home. I knew the seed of Love was
planted and a new relationship with God was born within me.
A sense of before unknown presence and feelings of awareness
made me know that there was change but as with any newborn,

understanding would come with time. I was like a fish out of water for the next nine months. Unsure of my next step ......though my choice willing. Giving my life and all its holdings into His care. A step by step walk, small revelation up small revelation, building block upon building block.

Revealing Himself to me through forgiveness and acceptance at the lowest point thus far in my life; a ruined marriage, failed relationships, lack of self-control; having drunk myself to oblivion more times than I care to recount, experimentation with drugs and sex. All attempts to look for meaningful love **in my own name** achieved absolutely nothing of lasting quality. Grateful for His forgiveness, spiritual reality of true Love, despite prior attempts of my own to find Love, planted my feet on the path that would lead to lasting relationship with a Love who would change my name, self -image, and give purpose to all of life.

Another step toward freedom; the ultimate step now taken I just needed to keep walking with Jesus, getting to know Him through obedience to His word, moving away from self-centeredness, learning to love myself and others the way He did. The Message version of the Bible says in Galatians 5 that this is the act of true freedom.

It is two sided, love oneself and love others as you would yourself. If we want to be free, we must do both. It isn't the easiest, but God doesn't give us the easy way out. The no discipline way, The painless way, The ideal Way. No, He teaches us to love everyday through opportunities to love both ourselves and others. It takes time and His perspective which he gives us as we grow in deeper surrender to Him; Loving Him more results in loving ourselves and others, it means becoming the

original we truly are and allowing others the same privilege without trying to get our own way all the time. It is obvious what kind of life develops out of trying to get our own way all the time: repetitive, loveless, cheap sex; a stinking accumulation of mental and emotional garbage; frenzied and joyless grabs for happiness; trinket gods; magic show religion; paranoid loneliness; cut-throat competition; all consuming-yet-never-satisfied wants; a brutal temper; an impotence to love or be loved; divided homes and divided lives; small minded and lop-sided pursuits; the vicious habit of depersonalizing everyone into a rival; uncontrolled and uncontrollable addictions; ugly parodies of community. I could go on.

But what happens when we live God's way? He brings gifts into our lives, much the same way fruit appears in an orchard-things like affection for others, exuberance about life, serenity, we develop a willingness to stick with things, a sense of compassion in the heart, and a conviction that a basic holiness permeates things and people. We find ourselves involved in loyal commitments, not needing to force our way in life, able to marshal and direct our energies wisely.

Legalism is helpless in bringing this about; it only gets in the way. Among those who belong to Christ everything connected with getting our own way and mindlessly responding to what everyone else calls necessities is killed off for good-crucified.

The amount of true love we have received or not received is directly connected to our individual amount of self-centeredness. How quickly we learn to receive true Love is determined by our willingness to surrender self to the crucifixion of our worldly soul values. I cannot stress this point too much. We must be the ones who give permission to God to search us by the light of His Holy Spirit according to His word to us in the Holy Scriptures.

Overcoming self-centeredness requires looking to Christ for vision away from ourselves and toward others. There is no need to explain why you do act, if the act is within the realm of Love and has been given to you through prayers of submission to the will of Holy Spirit. Even acts done in hope of thanks and appreciation are self-centered, for Christ taught in Matthew 6:1-34, highlighting verse 1, "Beware of practicing your righteousness before other people in order to be seen by them for you will have no reward from your Father who is in heaven."

By this crossroad in my life I had moved back into the house, the one on the now paved path, the one my Father chose. Divorced, my home would be a stable factor for future years of growth. Counseling changed my thinking processes. Encouraged by my counselor to think about finishing bachelor's degree work in Business Administration, lead me to discuss the possibility with my father. Returning full-time would mean leaving the company and my only source of income. Father thought it was a good plan and offered to help me accomplish it. I procured a real estate license in effort to supplement my father's generosity. Ben would be cared for by one of my parent's long-time friends, Momma G. Invitation to learn the real estate business came through a woman from my counseling group and involved resort property in Horseshoe Bay, TX. My confidence, in selling, was not high, because my self was not sure about much, having left my old self at the cross for transformation everything was opportunity toward new life. She thought a trip to visit that property would help give an experience relatable to perspective clients. Coinciding with this, business course work in college began to lose appeal. I began seeking God's direction for possible change of major, considering a Bible School as an option. I was enjoying two of my gen-ed requirements; Sociology and Marriage and Family. I prayed and waited until I knew that I was to stay on at my college but move to a major in Social Service. These two classes introduced others who engaged me in learning more about walking out the Christian faith. New Perspective came when I met Tim and Twila, who became new Christian friends. Both in the same major, Twila surprisingly lived less than a half mile from home, practicing her faith with church and family in my own community. Tim, lived in the dorm and was part of a Christian vocal group, 4-Him, an on-campus ministry. On walks through the quad we shared our life experience and I received their words of needed insight to living out faith in Christ. One day conversation confronted issues of flirtatious actions; my response to guys. Words of correction were hard to hear and receive for their intended purpose. I had to think about my actions and contemplate the truth of what was being said, trusting that my friends had my best interest at heart and their experience in faith had given them insight to help me. Trusting people to have my good at heart was not something I did. That is not saying that people did not have my good at heart sometimes, but I just hadn't understood their actions were with that intent. My wounds were gaping and bleeding, causing reaction, not well thought out response. For the first time I became aware of how others perceived my spirit and heard wisdom of possible consequences. God wanted me to stop those behaviors so I would no longer be seeking careless attention and putting others in a position to hurt. Caring friendship was new to me outside the realm of counseling. My defensive ways of the past kept friendship at a distance safe from more hurts. I liked the ability to hear and learn new responses; based in telling the truth in the love of Christ, it gave a feeling of security and sureness about relationship.

One evening, lying on the sofa, engaged in phone conversation with Tim, a voice interrupted," Susan, I am answering your prayers". Without a doubt, it was the Lord's voice as it seemed all at once gentle, strong, and assuring. With one sentence, He spoke my name with a love I had not before experienced. That voice and moment I decided to leave behind any previous names I had been called and chose to be called "Susan". I had prayed for one man to share my life with spiritually. I thought that He meant Tim. However, I came to realize it was to be Jesus, Him and Him first.

Tim and I dated for a few months. He tolerated sinful unregenerate behaviors yet untransformed by Love. My new status; babe in Christ. I appreciated Tim's truthful insight as we cooked a meal. Asking if there was anything he could do to help, I responded he could peel the potatoes. Clearly, I thought he was doing it wrong and told him how to do it. He spoke "there's more than one way to peel a potato". God was speaking too. I would have to learn the lesson of allowing differences for other's ways to do things which weren't sin, only different from my own way. Inherited self-righteousness would have to go, and the love of God through Tim would help me clear the path to God's righteousness. Eventually unable to continue relationship, because my past was still leading me into sinful behavior, Tim knew to be wrong; feeling the conviction of his participation; our dating was ended. I did not yet share his ability to choose the righteous way and wanted to be angry with him for rejecting my immature sinful acts.

I would have to be shown through circumstances, behaviors not becoming of good relationship. Ending relationship with Tim broke my heart but choosing to see the outcome from God's perspective helped me to lay aside ruling emotions. Hurt and rejection caused me to break prior commitment to walk in a Spring fashion show that Tim had organized. God would not have it. I would be giving up growth and staying in my old ways, but God had me realize laying aside emotions to walk in Love was a lesson requiring tests in many opportunities. I apologized, asking to be reinstated as a model and did the show which was enormously enjoyable. Christ Won (1), Satan, 0!!

January, while still with Tim, but experiencing unrest, a conversation with my neighbor and friend revealed her initiative to begin church attendance at the local Bible Church. She thought it the right thing to do for herself and her girls. Not many months into the future her invitation to join her on Palm Sunday would bring my own decision to at least give it a try. My Lutheran upbringing reinforced church attendance, especially Easter and Christmas holidays. Deeply, desiring to expand my knowledge and experience of God caused consideration of her invitation. The mere size of the church, three times more people than my childhood church was enough to put fear into me. The fact that I was hearing a voice, some jokingly call the devil on your shoulder, telling me, "everyone knows your reputation!", because of small community added to my angst. However, stronger desire to change my life, made the possibility of overcoming fear, healthy in every way. The thought of Singing was a joy to my heart, stirring up good memories of childhood; singing in choir and mother/daughter duets of showtunes as she played the piano. I accepted her invitation for the first Sunday in March. Invited back the following week for Easter, I also accepted. The third week, though she would be out of town, she encouraged me to attend on my own. Unsettled fear of sitting alone was overcome and I walked through the doors on time to drop Ben in class and be seated for services by the usher. Carefully observing my surroundings, I noted a man out of my left vision, who while singing hymns, was "checking me out" with continual glances in my direction. As my discomfort grew, I planned my escape to follow the final notes of the last hymn. Running if possible, in the opposite direction so as not to risk an unwanted meeting. Quickly, as the hymn was ending, I would hurriedly put my book in the pew and gather my belongings during the last chorus. Backfiring and halted as I turned to execute my escape; all movement came to a sudden halt as half the church was also trying to vacate the sanctuary. I tried to avoid his approach by not looking his direction. I didn't look but he still approached and made his presence into "my space". Avoidance at this point was not an option. His bold greeting met me; announcing his name with outstretched hand. "Hi, I'm Gary, Gary Barr." Awkward! Small talk and watching for movement ahead were all I remember of that meeting. Thoughts bombarded my mind. How I could escape any involvement with another man? I was desperately trying to get free from promiscuity and failed relationship. I wasn't ready for another one.

Persistently waiting on any given Sunday after service, Gary would stand by the only exit from the Sunday School area to the parking lot. The only exit I knew and not wanting to be rude, friendly exchange was most unavoidable. His huge smile, with Bible tucked under arm, pleasantly evoked consistency every week breaking down resistance.

Coming the end of April, my visit to Texas for Real Estate was planned. I would have to make extended plans for Ben to stay with his father as it would be his arranged weekend to visit with his son. About a month ahead, open conversation to change the schedule by one night was met with denial due to his new wife's reluctance. Her birthday weekend had no time for Ben. Getting a babysitter wasn't an option for their evening celebration and my frustration with late pick-up, and no pick-ups, hit a peak. I expressed my anger with an ultimatum to either pick him up and get a sitter like a father would or take his lack of commitment to the next level. Addressing the effects of inconsistency in those moments ended with "If you are not going take him and be consistent. Please just don't bother to get him ever again. He doesn't need an absent father and disappointment." It is sad to say he chose the latter, but his continued use of alcohol and drugs was the one thing I did not wish Ben to observe, the divorce would be enough for him to deal with emotionally. Ben was just eighteen months old. I would make other arrangements for his care that weekend.

Traveling by myself, Texas was less than half the time to Hawaii. I had managed that trip and facing more fear didn't stop me. Gaining confidence in experiencing, hopeful it would be what I needed to help me succeed in real estate. The home market was consciously conflicting for me. Representing the seller and putting homes that had problems in a "good" light made me feel uncomfortable, like I was telling half-truths. Maybe new construction was my opportunity. Investors and agents shared a tour and dinner our first night on site. I met an investor from Alberta, Canada who was a successful contractor and investor. Attraction was mutual, his Ukrainian accent drew me into the soft flow of words, evoking emotion. Spending the rest of our time together; we fell hard and fast into planning a future together, talking every night long distance, planning a visit mid-June for him in PA. and us to Canada sometime later in the summer.

His strong character attracted me, and he treated me with tenderness and care, but then the impulsiveness of the moment does not always pave the way for solid foundations. His impulsive ways fed my own and we thought our future was to be married. Upon my return from Texas, Gary would remain faithful in his position, patiently walking me to the car, inquiring about happenings of my life. He asked if he could call me sometime. Responding with a business card and closed emotion, telling him of my involvement with Ron, I hoped it would be a put-off to him.

Long phone conversations to Canada every night after tucking Ben in bed fed the relationship fire, but all the while God was at work, teaching and imparting grace and wisdom through His word making me aware of my need for Him to be involved in my choices. I was being positioned to fully surrender everything I knew and come to a greater understanding of His transforming power. May 31, 1981 as the service ended with the singing of "Whiter than Snow", a hymn, which is a prayer, written by James Nicholson, at age 25, in the City of Brotherly Love, Philadelphia, PA. The prelude was played; singing began. With heartfelt prayerful agreement to his words, I made petition by the following entreaty.

Lord Jesus I long to be perfectly whole;
I want thee forever to live in my soul.
Break down every idol, cast out every foe;
Now wash me and I shall be whiter than snow.
Refrain Whiter than snow, yes whiter than snow.
Now wash me and I will be whiter than snow.

Lord Jesus let nothing unholy remain,
Apply Thine own blood and extract ev'ry stain;
To get this blest cleansing, I all things forgo-
Now wash me and I shall be whiter than snow.

Refrain

Lord Jesus look down from Thy throne in the skies
And help me to make a complete sacrifice.
I give up myself and whatever I know,
Now wash me and I shall be whiter than snow.

Around this point a flood of tears accompanied my final pleas.

Refrain

Lord Jesus, for this I most humbly entreat,
I wait blessed Lord, at thy crucified feet.
By faith for my cleansing, I see thy blood flow,
Now wash me, and I shall be whiter than snow.

Refrain

Lord Jesus, Thou seest I patiently wait,
Come now, and within me a new heart create;

To those who sought Thee, thou never sadist "No".
Now wash me and I shall be whiter than snow.

Refrain

The blessing of faith, I receive from above;
O glory! My soul is made perfect in love;
My prayer has prevailed, and this moment I know,
The blood is applied, I am whiter than snow.

Refrain

During the last verse amidst tears, a supernatural washing occurred from the top of my head to the bottom of my feet. Palpable, unmistakable and as real as anything I had ever experienced. Supernatural water, of the Holy Spirit, flowed like a river, entering my space; answering my cries for salvation. Answering my pleas, washing away years of hurt, rejection, pain and guilt. I felt New. My thinking turned in new direction, a feeling like His hand reached inside rotating my brain, setting it in line as originally intended at His conception of me. Awe and wonder filled my being. Leaving the sanctuary, a new person, I arrived at my car to leave. Normally the first thing I did was light up a smoke but today was not the same. I noticed a difference. Surprised and thankful, he had taken my desire and addiction to cigarettes; a two pack a day habit. He knew it was necessary. There were much deeper strongholds to overcome and smoking, a major hindrance, removed, so the rest could be uncovered. Overwhelming gratefulness, welling up within, sold out to knowing this Great Love for which I had searched and longed for all the days of my life. It compared to nothing I had received on Christmas morning, Birthdays, etc. The love I was feeling, felt complete. I never wanted to go back to the darkness and bondage of my previous experience. Passion for everyone to hear what He had done; I wasted no time opening my mouth about what I received in every joyful encounter with others. Wanting everyone to experience Him the way I did. I was "on fire" as Twila put it during a recent conversation some 35+ years later. Making sparks fly was taking on a new meaning.

One summer encounter with a fellow high school cheerleader, a well-meaning believer who questioned me and had been there when I was made substitute, after hearing of my new testimony questioned, "Isn't it wonderful to let Go and let God?" Of course, I did not know exactly what that meant. I walked away, pondering her words through infantile understanding. Lack of maturity caused thoughts to follow the path of "If God does it all then what do I have to do": essentially translating as "nothing", putting me on the sofa in depression. God would not let me there. Hebrews 5:13-14 AMP gave me some understanding and a push forward to step in faith toward maturity. Verse 13. For everyone who continues to feed on milk is obviously inexperienced and unskilled in the doctrine of righteousness (of conformity to divine will in purpose, thought and action), for he is a mere infant. [not able to talk yet] 14. But solid food is of full-grown men (and women [my addition]), for those whose senses are trained by practice to discriminate and distinguish between what is moral good and noble and what is evil and contrary either to divine or human law. This lesson was for the more mature of understanding. Letting go of hurts, woundedness, unforgiveness and experience through continual submission was letting God have control of the outcomes of the future. Now the struggle has transformed and though depression will always be my enemy, God has taught me how to fight unto victory, using the weapons of my faith.

How do I convey the passion of my relationship: His working to make me all I can be in Him? Sharing my faith with others? Getting to the place of peace and rest; yet still wanting more of Him? The complexity of the struggle is the push and pull of His love working to cleanse the old nature, moving our being into depths where only His grace (favor) can take us, gained by continual submission of the mind, will and emotions to His will. In accomplishing this process, eventually, the old nature of the soul no longer, due to discipline, presents itself as a choice. You have been made new in His likeness, but then, even the understanding is: You must continue on the journey in submission to experience more of Him.

Relationships used to steer my path were part of His plan to bring me to maturity. I would learn to embrace the good, the bad and the ugly with passion, obedience and submission moving onward to becoming. This was not my last struggle with depression. Breakthrough would take 11 years of discipline to see deliverance in that arena. Catherine Brown states the mission of our calling so well in a prophetic word given in 2007 on The Elijah List website. "When our hearts enter the blessedness of divine romance with Christ, we are released to a lifetime of effective mission. To be carried in His heart is to carry His heart of mercy to pursue people and cities until they are delivered from judgement of sin and rebellion, and delivered into a loving, living faith relationship with God. Our mission must flow from being undone by His Love; for without it our mission becomes merely works." Transformation and mission happen simultaneously when the relationship with Christ is in the correct perspective.

Continuing she states, "His love is our preparation causing holy devastation to our flesh to produce purity and divine desperation in us, to continually seek Him with all our hearts and make His unquenchable, agape Love known throughout the world. We are revived for mission."

I was rejoicing inwardly and outwardly, relishing a Love I had never experienced or even imagined possible. This was the Love of my Life whom I had searched for in all the wrong places, but He knew exactly how bring me into his embrace, causing me to surrender everything into His care. The very same night of my transformation, my "love" from Canada was taken aback by my Love from above. In extreme dismay, after my flourishing, emphatic description of the day's events, Ron could only acknowledge the new me: "Who is this I am talking too? It certainly isn't the girl I met in Texas!" True words spoken, I quickly agreed because I just wasn't and was never going to be that girl he met in Texas. Insatiable hunger to know Jesus caused me to spend many hours seeking him in the Word, prayer, teaching and fellowship that summer. My radio was tuned to the Christian station most of the day, with my Bible open to look up the scripture being taught. Plans for Ron to fly had already been made and his hope that my passion would wane and one day we would marry motivated him. His arrival, only a short couple of weeks away, had me determined to hold fast to Jesus, resisting all intimacy of any other kind. The enemy of my soul was not going to give up the ground he had gained so easily and would use whatever charms he knew to weaken me in that determination. Ron was not giving up, though I expressly spoke our differences could not be resolved at this time. All the way to Philadelphia International Airport the discussion centered on compatibility with no agreement. Ben and I were to visit Alberta in July. Tickets purchased, I was willing to cut the losses, but His insistence, pleasing manner and Ukrainian accent, melted any resolve to resist. He was likable in many areas but not a believer. A stronghold gained through intimacy and my ignorance allowed access to my soul. My last hope of avoidance came in the form of an airline strike as I gave up my plans to God's will, praying that if He wanted me to go then the strike would end by the time we were to leave, if not I was happy to remain at home.

How could this be? The airline strike ended just in time for our flights to take place. Stunned that God could allow this considerably unwanted avenue to open only to make way for plans, greater in purpose. He does this. He allows challenges. We must learn to make good choices when they come. Upon arrival, I accompanied Ron on a ride some distance away for a business meeting. Inviting me to accompany him into the meeting, my insecurities took the forefront. I was out of my familiar surroundings and coping, I declined, waiting in the car. Our return trip back to his place assured me that I would not be tying the knot with Ron, adamantly revealing his desire for a marriage contract to which I emphatically replied, "Well then, I guess you won't be marrying me because my next marriage will be based in trust!" Back to more discussion on getting together...

By the third day of my three weeks stay, I was in melt down mode. Wanting to return home, calling on my BFF for support, surprisingly, I became very aware why God had sent me on this trip. His plan was to show me Tim's perspective of our relationship and my errant actions which caused its end. I could clearly see myself in Ron's behavior and it wasn't a pretty sight. I had not seen how I had "dragged Tim into the dirt", beguiling him with temptations that were against his beliefs and disrespecting him. Now I was on the other side of the fence and I did not like how it felt pushy and compromising. God was with me and speaking loudly to once again transform my past.

Conflicting views of life and pressure to fit them together was coming from Ron, like trying to put a square peg in a round hole. Tempers flared and I cried. My insistence broke through and he realized the relationship just wasn't going to work, but knowing I had spent money, he convinced me without pressure to let him show me Alberta and some of its treasures. One of which was meeting his mother who spoke no English and lived in a one room house without running water or bath, heated by a wood stove. She was so happy and enjoyed her life on an expanse of farmland where she herself worked a small plot on 3000 acres and kept herself busy with a very simple life. Blessed to eat her amazing Ukrainian finger size cabbage rolls along with horseback riding will be remembered as the highlights of my trip.

Upon my arrival home, I could not wait to ask Tim's forgiveness. Hoping for reconciliation, wasting no time, I traveled the following weekend to NJ, where his mother would direct me to his work to seek his forgiveness and share my understanding. He was able to break. I explained to him my realization in Canada. The convictions my sin imposed upon him and need for confession. Most of all, my hope that He could see the visible signs of work done by God; that I was different. I am sure he prayed for me and sure he was glad to see answers. His excitement for my growth was evident and forgiveness granted. We had been apart in viewpoint. Now we were closer. Maybe we could start over.

Sunday following, we returned to church. "Gary, Gary Barr", stood once again waiting at the doors, determined as ever to continue pursuit. Ron was no longer. Hope was for Tim, and then there was Gary, who just didn't seem my type. However, I didn't say no to a request by phone to take me to dinner the following Saturday. Time drew closer, though I was no closer to any inclination this relationship would work either. Answering the door, He stood well dressed and groomed, which certainly was a positive. Opening the car door for me (another positive), we drove the 81 express to a steakhouse in Harrisburg. Menus in hand, a request for drink orders came. Declining any alcohol, spurring conversation on individual beliefs; sharing with him my experience and family bent toward overindulgence. He asked what I wanted to order and proceeded to give my order to the waitress. I was impressed. My father would have done the same. He was scoring points! Before we arrived, I did notice and liked the look of his strong, workworn hands, an indication of a work ethic. At dinner I enjoyed his smile and told him so. Nearing completion of our meal he declared observation. "Boy, you sure eat a lot! I have never taken a girl out who ate as much as you do." I wanted to shrink under the seat in embarrassment. However, explaining Ron had encouraged me to eat more in Canada because he didn't like "thin" girls was my truthful response. It didn't take much encouragement to eat more because food had become a comfort, as a child, during stressful times. My weight usually fluctuated between indulgences and dieting.

The drive home held questions that probed my beliefs. His most truthful observance, spoken with emphasis, and received with shock was "Boy, you really are a hardcore Christian!" Quick and just as emphatically I retorted, "yes and it isn't going to change!" So, if you want to accept it okay and if not, okay again. Most ready for this date to be over, I would have to think about all that happened and wonder if his pursuit would lessen. After picking Ben up at my friend's house, we came to my front door to say our goodbyes. A thank you with a sisterly peck on the cheek left Gary quizzically looking bewildered. I hadn't extended an invitation to come inside. The brash words of his observations and a desire to lessen temptation left me cautious and not desiring further time with him. Church services the next day required getting Ben to bed then taking time to process the date.

His persistent pursuit continued the next day and on Tuesday night the phone rang. "Hi, this is Gary. Are you going to be home? I was wondering if I might stop by on my way home from my mother's house in Lawn?" I said yes to both but had no intention of entertaining him in the house where I knew the enemy could play on my past weaknesses of emotion and promiscuity. Quickly, I got Ben ready for bed. Within a twenty-minute window also building a campfire; settling on this location as a safe place for conversation. Little did I realize, he loved campfires, throwing fuel on his affection and giving him hope. An avid hunter and outdoorsman, he was pleasantly amazed. We both enjoyed this type of atmosphere. Managing by night's end to set up a second date for the following Saturday which would include Ben. He was winning approval. Ben's inclusion was important to any future relations. A local juried art festival, held yearly on the third week of August, would be our destination. Gary was attentive to both Ben and me. Turning my thoughts and prayer to the future of Ben's needs for attentive good man who could be a good father if we were to ever remarry. I had hopes of becoming a good wife and mother, I was interested in learning to see these roles from God's perspective. It was important knowledge to attain if I was to avoid past mistakes. I was grateful for the Holy Spirit.

He was always with me and made me aware of truth and error, highlighting the words of 1John 1: 26,27: 26. I write this to you with reference to those who would deceive you [seduce you and lead you astray]. 27. But as for you, the anointing (the sacred appointment, the unction) which you received from Him abides [permanently] in you; [so] then you have no need that anyone should instruct you. But just as his anointing teaches you concerning everything and is true and is not falsehood, so you must abide in [live in, never depart from,] Him [being rooted in Him, knit to Him], just as [His anointing] has taught you to do. One of His helpers was my grandma.

Teaching me, my grandma would often quote from Romans 3:4. Her words translated from scripture? (Romans 3:4) "Call every man a liar but my word is truth." Truth keeps us from deception. Deception is a state of being that can only be seen by those not under the same deception or revealed by prayer request to reveal it. "Am I deceived?" is a question which should be asked of the Lord, if we are in confusion about an issue. The answer should be waited upon and action avoided until received. Waiting was difficult for me especially because all my life my emotions lead me by impulse.

Now I had to learn the word of God and let it be the light for my path. Grandma's support was priceless, she was all too happy her prayers for my salvation had been heard. I had one family member who was happy for my conversion. She had made the decision to follow Jesus at the age of fifty. A prayer warrior, she saw six of her children make the decision as well. Her counsel and prayers undergirded me. On one night, Ben awakened me with screams of terror. Quickly, in fear, running to his room next door, I saw him sitting up with eyes focused intently on something only he seemed to be able to see. Again, speaking authoritatively the name of Jesus, God's peace came to us immediately. Shaken and wanting support I did not hesitate to call Grandma at midnight. Her reassuring words and prayers enabled our return to rest. All these circumstances encouraged not giving up the journey even though the challenges to my commitment sometimes scared me. My new relationship with Gary was one of those challenges.

Dating progressed, yet in my heart, a hope for reconciliation with Tim was still underlying as I waited for his return to college that Fall. Perceiving my desire, after a few weeks of dating Gary and conversation with Tim, I realized reconciliation wasn't going to happen on a deeper level. Tim said I was already involved with someone else and I should continue that direction. Disappointment pushed me. Impulsively diving into the next level of intimacy with Gary, ultimately too much, too soon, guilty of sin and trying to undo damages, I retreated to God's standard and forgiveness. I had fallen from righteousness and deeply needed and wanted to feel good about my actions. It was difficult to come to agreement, but I found forgiveness and grace to avoid intimacy on that level until marriage.

A fall trip to see the beauty of the changing leaves to upstate PA, exposed emotions and memories still imposing themselves on the new canvas of my life. This is the stuff of our flesh where the soul resides, and Christ teaches us to deny toward the greater life of the Spirit. Wanting to be honest and upfront, I shared with Gary my internal emotion, in hope of empathy, encouragement, release of memories; my thoughts and words, grounds for deepening understanding and compassion. However, I was surprised at his angry response of jealousy and misunderstanding. Attempts failed to reassure him I was only trying to get over the past, causing conflict. Expressing no desire to return to that relationship, only to share struggle of loss and the memories of what I learned about relationship were overriding time which should have been focused on us. Return to familiar settings; facing the past to leave it with new perspective so we could move into our future was what I had in mind.

Leaving the past behind would become a theme of growth. It hadn't been too many months since my commitment to follow Christ, I was fearfully awakened by a heavy pressure on my chest, making me unable to breathe normally or make even a small sound. Opening my eyes and struggling to get a grasp on what was happening, I opened my eyes to a horrible apparition in the corner of my room. I surmised it was the devil himself, and no he was not red and carrying a pitchfork. With an immediate response I attempted to cry out the name of Jesus because I knew the word instructed believers to resist the devil and he would flee. Trying to call out the name of Jesus and get breathe at the same time seemed impossible and the fear gripped me ruthlessly as the pressure increased and the struggle to gain even a small breath remained out of possibility. His Name seemed to remain stuck in my head, being repeated but unable to escape to my voice. However, after what seemed like a long time of inability and struggle, my voice released, loudly declaring "Jesus!"; in that moment of breath and release the evil presence departed. Relieved it was over, I prayed enthusiastically to thank the Lord for His deliverance. I was very aware I had an enemy who was angered by my decision and actions to follow Jesus. The devil was going to try to scare me back to the dark side. He was a formidable enemy, I called grandma.

God undergirded me once again with Grandma's support. She was 80 years old at the time and had decided to follow Jesus herself at the age of fifty. A prayer warrior herself, it didn't matter when I called at midnight when another spiritual attack came. She reassured me with prayer, and I was able to return to rest in my soul. We were spending a lot of time, sharing Jesus. I was enjoying this new level of relationship with my grandma, who had always shown me love, just not approval. Now it seemed she was approving of my actions too.

Thanksgiving was approaching, and Gary and I were declaring love for one another. We would share the day in celebration with family and on Saturday before he left for Buck hunting with family, he would plan to spend the entire day with me including shopping and dinner. Gary was making a good wage with Bethlehem Steel Corporation and had done so for the past 11 years. Saturday arrived, and his plans included an hour trip to the outlet center in Reading. He indulged and encouraged some purchases for me of clothing, knowing by now that I love to shop and love nice clothing. Driving through familiar towns on our way home, we stopped in the town where he had spent most of his school years, at the Kumm Esse Diner ("Come Eat", Pennsylvania Dutch language). It had been one of his favorite haunts as a child. They served homestyle Pennsylvania Dutch food and pies the like of which was unmatched anywhere else in the county. We enjoyed our meal and afterward picked Ben up at my parent's. Settling on the couch for snuggling, he popped the question "Will you marry me?" Surprised, I answered yes and the following week after his return we would shop for a ring.

Just before Christmas we would take Ben and baking supplies up to my parent's Log home in the mountains for a picture-perfect weekend of cookie baking and snow. Seemingly, we would have a good family. Plans to marry were set for the following June with a two-week honeymoon to follow, one for just Gary and I and one for the family. The church where we met and still attended did not share our belief that we could remarry, making it clear they were not going to accept our decision which I knew was contrary to what I had earnestly studied, prayed and listened to God's answer for us. I had not really known God had a detailed plan for marriage. To me it was just something you do when you come of age. His forgiveness made it possible to remarry. Is it always permissible? Time spent seeking scripture with a prayerful attitude before such a monumental decision is vital. Gary was under the freedom to remarry through his prior spouse's unfaithfulness. We would seek counsel from other mature believers and eventually settle on seeking out my high school classmate who pastored a church in the little village only a hop skip and a jump from my house. Condemnation and guilt were not compatible with what we thought the Bible conveyed about love, grace and forgiveness. Believing there was hope for a relationship built on the word and work of the Lord for His glory and our future, there was freedom to marry again.

Dave Hess pastored the small fellowship about 2 miles from my house. On a Sunday, we decided to visit. Fellowship was welcoming and there were people we knew. Dave and Sheri greeted at the end of service, we approached to huge hugs and smiles. Dave said he was shocked as he saw me be seated, almost falling out of the pulpit. Through conversation, I would find out he had been praying for my salvation for the past eight years. Now I was shocked! Saved in his early high school years, he attended a James Robison youth rally in Hershey, PA. James put out a challenge. "If you really want to see God move, I want you to go back into your high school and look around at the students, don't pick the first one you see, but seriously consider who would be the least likely to follow Christ and pick them. Then pray faithfully until you see them come to Christ."

Dave chose me! He had seen firsthand my rebellious, promiscuous lifestyle with a front row seat. Well, a rearview seat as my last name was alphabetically in front of his and we shared some classes which made him privy to my outspoken escapades and in between class antics. My disrespect, foul mouth, and untamed behaviors had won me the spot of top choice for Dave's prayers. I could hardly believe someone would care so deeply as to make sure I would know the Love of the Father, who amazingly could turn me from my wicked ways. Dave will always hold a very special place in my heart. Who knows if I would even be alive if he had not dedicated himself through prayer? The love of Christ was drawing us. In the coming months, the decision was made, this fellowship would become our new church home. Dave and

Sheri had passion for the ways of the Lord. Teaching through their example of worshipful lifestyle: God would lay the foundation of small group gatherings as a must for growth. Sunday worship just wasn't enough to build lasting relationship. Spending time getting to know people is the only way you can know what they need. Dave and Sheri wanted to know us and care for us. His counsel was valuable.

Our premarital counseling in the new year uncovered more of my instability and unsureness of entering marriage a second time. I did not take lightly the prospect of remarrying for I had decided there would be no divorce option. Now I had Christ by His Holy Spirit to confront me and help me succeed in God's plan, but I needed to allow my soul's desires to know with finality Gary was the one. Unsure, I put the wedding on hold, causing Gary great stress. I had to pray and know for sure.

Seeking a definitive yes from the Lord was our desire and the delay was not to be. We stuck with our plan for June though changed the honeymoon through New England's Bed and Breakfasts, because we had cancelled all reservations during the hold. During the same timeframe, I was also seeking truth about the baptism of the Holy Spirit. There seemed to me, two viewpoints were presenting themselves and I wanted truth. One stated that the Holy Spirit came with a commitment to Christ and tongues left with the last of the twelve apostles. The other was that it was still received at commitment but that a baptism of the Holy Spirit was taught in the scriptures which was evidence of the new birth and a gift to help us pray. I had been water baptized shortly after my surrender, but now I read about speaking in tongues being the evidence of the baptism of the Spirit. Something I did not possess. I was not going to just unreservedly accept what people said. I was looking for God's perspective. What was reality? I would continue praying for an answer until I was sure I had one.

The book of Acts (the account of the first experiences of the New Testament church) written during the time of the birthing of the Church after Christ's ascension would provide an accurate picture. Again, Grandma encouraged me to seek truth quoting Romans 3:3-4 AMP. What if some did not believe and were without faith: Does their lack of faith and their faithlessness nullify and make ineffective and void the faithfulness of God and His fidelity [to His Word]? 4. By no means! Let God be found true though every human being is false and a liar, as it is written, that you may be justified and shown to be upright in what you say, and prevail when you are judged [by sinful men]. Learning that I was also one who was false and needed to be changed by the truth made this word a pillar in my foundation allowing it to draw me to His inspired inerrant Word of Truth for answers to my questions of faith. He would clarify it in time.

Clarity was on the way. God was answering my prayers. The day of my wedding in June, my salon experience would be unforgettably powerful. Doors to the drying room were closed after we entered, no one else was there. Sonia and I sat across a vanity where she would do my manicure. Noticing I was wearing a gold cross spurred a question. In her lovely Korean accent, she asked, "Are you a born-again believer? You receive Jesus as savior?" Joyfully and emphatically declaring "Yes!" Continuing to question, "You receive, baptism in Holy Spirit?" Amazed and pleased, I hoped she could shed light on my inquiry of the Lord about her own experience. Responding, 'No, but I have been praying about that and would like to know more." She began, "Baptism in Holy Spirit give you power to be witness for God." The presence of the Lord was in this place manifesting in new ways. I have always used the analogy of a marble glass covered cheese dome to describe the atmosphere of protected, anointed conversation and place we were sharing that day. It was real as anything else in the room. God totally enabled a set apart time for me to hear her teaching and testimony.

Sonia shared she had been working for a trucking company on the loading docks, moving from the streets Korea to California with her serviceman husband, after being homeless most of her childhood. Eventually she landed in PA. A mother of two teenage girls, divorced and again without support, they journeyed eastward to PA. Her heritage of witchcraft, she was to be the next family high priestess. She described herself as tough and mean and nasty, fitting in well with the boys on the dock. Under the rule of drugs, nobody wanted to mess with her. There was, however, the man in the booth, on the dock, who shared with Sonia about the Love of Christ. Drawn by his kindness they visited regularly on breaks or just in passing. On one night, she fell to the floor, passed out unconscious from overdose. As she lay, she had an encounter with Jesus. Jesus gave her a choice. Her life was required of Him. She could serve him and be healed and delivered from her evil lifestyle or die that very night, spending eternity in Hell. She chose Jesus and was delivered into God's Kingdom that night. But not unchallenged in her decision, her house, not far into her future, was burnt to the ground, the only thing left was her picture of Jesus hanging on the wall surrounded with a remnant of the evidence of smoke.

My heart was being touched in ways not known or experienced, evoking a reality of God. Tears flowing down my cheeks as my heart was happy to see and hear miraculous work happening today: not only when Christ was on the earth but now. Her life was evidence to me that God's power was real and by faith it could change lives. Relaying that sometime after that, while worshipping on a Sunday evening at Grace Chapel, she heard a voice repeating over and over the instruction to "Go check into the hospital for a rest." Skeptical and not wanting to do something so out of the ordinary if it was not the voice of God, she afterward sought the elders for discernment through prayer. They would agree, it was the Holy Spirit. She **should** obey. She **would** obey. Driving immediately to the medical center, where Doctors and Nurses would inquire as to why she had come, to which she only replied, "For a rest". No one understood, as they had never had anyone who just wanted to check in for a rest. Don't people go on vacation for rest, check into a hotel? Not a hospital. Numbers of staff, one after the other, were unsuccessful at getting any other response, so after midnight, concluded she must be delusional and admitted to the psychiatric unit. She would come to understand, this was God's choice for her "rest", as over the next two weeks she would discover thirteen born again Christians who needed spiritual healing. God used her background of witchcraft knowledge to show dark evil spirits that kept these people from freedom. Bitterness, anger, past sin, each holding prison one of God's children. He wanted to set them free and use Sonia as his vessel. Recounting each case to me, details and victory of healing, my tears were non-stop. Nails complete, I had a become knitted with this new sister in Christ. There was immediate love and desire to continue getting to know one another and the looks of surprise as we exited the room were quizzical. As I left, she placed in my hand a book by Gloria Copeland on the Holy Spirit and you. I in turn left her with an invite to our wedding. Short notice prevented her attendance but not her future friendship in the days and months and years to come.

What a wedding gift from Father! I was ready, body, soul and spirit, to walk the aisle in my handmade cream lace tea length dress fashioned by Grandma and me; a replica of one seen in a current bridal magazine, costing ten times the price I paid for the lace. Receiving time and memories creating it with my Grandma were priceless, making it worth so much more. Our venue to exchange vows? My childhood home, surrounded with family, and a few friends was perfect. Even if pouring rain made the dining room, instead of the patio, the site for our exchange of vows. Accompanied by harp played by Dave's sister, I felt beautiful in the light of all that God had done to prepare me for this moment when my life would be committed to loving Gary till death do us part. The ceremony, interrupted by a ringing phone and some humor from Dave about "What God wants to build into this marriage is telephone answering service, brought laughter and relaxation to an otherwise serious commitment. Words from song of Solomon brought intimate thoughts of the love we share with one another and Christ. Family and friends worked three days to prepare the delectable buffet, with freshly picked local chocolate covered strawberry's and a tiered flowered confection of cake by our favorite local baker, along with salads and tea sandwiches. A memorable day to say the least, we were blessed with all the goodness of God. I hoped it would be the standard for our life. Off we drove into" Happily ever After" …

Turning bad to good is God's specialty: I saw him doing this with my life. People hurt emotionally, physically and spiritually. Life is tough and even tougher if you don't understand how it got that way in the first place. The mind of a child cannot conceive of the effects of choices made for them. Some choices are not ours, others are, and we must come to understand the difference and make the choice to cooperate with God to transform choices that had negative consequences. Discerning wisdom enables us to view our life from God's perspective, simplifies decisions. Not easy but simple. Truth will always be truth, but the sight adjustment necessary to hit God's standards requires giving him freedom to speak truth to our heart. The part of us created to sense right from wrong. His mission is to transform us into sons and daughters, filled with life, and fulfilling purpose. So many of us wonder aimlessly, following others and their desires for us, as we seek acceptance, love and satisfaction. I just wanted somebody to understand who I am. It took a long time to realize God was the only one who could fully do that and given permission He would transform me with that understanding through His mighty word and power. It would take over two decades of growth to reach the point of experiencing relationships in which I felt understood.

Learning to perceive God's hand in all the years I lived, only became possible within our relationship. His Omniscience (all knowing) allowed my perception to view changes and events in my life from His intended purpose. Guidelines set in His word told me how to become who he always intended. My being unaware of all the details did not thwart his plans. It did however require surrender and trust, like falling backward off a platform into the arms of someone waiting to catch me. One plan I saw in conjunction with the desire for freedom, had come in the reading of *The Family Nobody Wanted* by Helen Doss. Though it had been about 15 years since I had read that book, my eyes were only opened to see how God had planted seeds for my future after my new birth. Helen and her pastor husband, lived in California, in the 1940's. Struggling to conceive, she seeks fulfillment through adoption of mixed-race children. In the intro, Mary Battenfield, says of Helen, "Thus, *The Family Nobody Wanted* suggests the ways in which people of different races and cultures are both the same and different, reminding us that we are all part of one race: The Human race despite differences physical ability or color. Helen's family celebrates her children's individual cultures and differences. Conforming my view of culture like unto Helen's as something to be celebrated, along with a desire to see people free to be, my vision could now see how God had shaped me for his purpose in the future. Reinforcing within me the equality of all people and exposing injustice and prejudice to act in faith by influencing my choices in relationship to people. Compassion stirred by the Doss's twelve children from varied backgrounds, both emotional and physical, living in our culture under the U.S. Constitution which declares life, liberty and the pursuit of happiness for all men living according to the laws of the nation and respect for authority, stemming from God motivated me even at the age of 9.

Now as a young adult, my heart was being shaped by influences known and unknown, past and present, with desire to live my life as a godly influence increased, under the now known guidance of God. My weaknesses and imperfections fully submitted to be shaped with more definition so He could use me to accomplish whatever he could for his purposes through me. Only three months into "happily ever after" frontline spiritual battles evidenced themselves in our lives.

August that summer, we were contemplating joining their fellowship permanently and they extended an invitation for the Jesus Festival at Agape Farm in Mt. Union. Camping, along with common meals, prepared the way to solidify our decision, as talk, laughter and growth made us part of the family. Morning, afternoon and evening, all would worship and learn from more mature teachers about living the Christian life. On one evening, an invitation to receive the baptism of the Holy Spirit was given, I saw this as answered prayer. If we wanted to receive, we were to go down front for laying on of hands and prayer. Not long after we walked forward, I received my gift of tongues with great joy, anticipating how to apply it by faith. I had been seeking this for months. God answers in His perfect time, not ours. God says, do not despise the day of small beginnings, so I would begin small by practical use and continued learning.

September saw me fighting sickness, of a nature I had not known prior. Pain was excruciating and a call to my doctor necessity. The call to the Doctor brought dismay. They would only be able to see me the following Monday, the unbearable pain was more than I could stand and pleaded for an immediate visit. To tolerate this extreme pain for five days, yet alone, not know diagnosis, my emphatic pleas opened the door that day. The diagnosis? An incurable disease that I would endure the rest of my life, however not life threatening. My thoughts immediately were," Well you don't know Jesus." He's in the healing business.

He had raised the dead, made the blind to see and took stripes for my healing. This was not too difficult for Him. To Him is where I would go. James 5:14-15 would give direction for my next steps. "Is anyone among you sick? He should call the church elders (the spiritual guides). And they should pray over him anointing him with oil in the Lord's name. 15. And the prayer [that is] of faith will save him who is sick, and the Lord will restore him; and if he has committed sins, he will be forgiven. AMP

In summer months a friend invited me to attend her fellowship on Sunday evenings, where I would seek prayers of faith. The doctor had given no hope of freedom, but I knew my God WAS hope. Prescribed medicine only added excruciating pain, so I threw it in the waste can and used what natural remedy I had available, battling through the painful symptoms by seeking Jesus hand. After all, as Hebrews 13:8 states, He is same yesterday, today, and forever. He did not change His mind about wanting to heal those who believe. Unable to drive due to the symptoms, my very good friend would take me to Victory Chapel. Approaching Erma, a woman elder, teaching that night, with my request, she told me they would pray with laying on of hands following teaching. Waiting in weakness, and longing anticipation on the front row pew, I sank lower and lower until reclined. Feelings of sickness, moment by moment, were making it impossible to remain upright, eventually landing my body horizontal on the pew. I needed help even to walk the short distance to the alter, where I knelt, so weak yet believing Jesus would do what he does. He does say when I am weak, He is strong! Encircled by His love, believers connected by the laying on of hands, their position forming an unbroken circle of God's energy and power, prayers began; native and spiritual tongues raised in petition for my wellness. The chorus of unity went to the heavens, I was waiting in silence but agreement for God's response. A breakthrough word came from a Native American brother, "Because you have been faithful to seek me, I will heal her."; at that very moment I felt His power pushing the sickness out through my body and replacing it with His health and peace. Rising to my feet in thankful praises. Rejoicing spread among the brethren as I relayed testimony of healing. Amazement at my deliverance, I could not have done it without my faithful family. He proved to me that His word is true and that putting my faith in action allowed for Him to respond. His good report of healing lifted confidence among the faithful. I now knew him as Savior, Healer, and Deliverer. I would declare it! Though I received my healing, the enemy was waiting in the background to come forth with his plan to make me try to believe it wasn't real: repeating over and over this lie trying to overcome me by weakening my faith. The next three weeks my belief and faith in the blood of Jesus would endure until the attacks of the enemy lies no longer bothered me and I entered the freedom of my healing completely.

The memory continues to bless me as almost forty years later, I have not experienced the painful symptoms again. My healing would take my faith to new levels and infuse me with even greater desire to tell of God's goodness. He was the same God of the scriptures. He longs to reveal Himself as the healer and Father of all. If we choose to believe in Him, then we can all experience life changes. I wanted to share His good report in hope that others would see and know that He is God. But if not, my confidence would remain in Christ.

My healing complete and on it's heals came the news we would receive a new child into our lives the following July. It was Fall now and October. October is a beautiful month, leaves changing, temperatures fair, and all seemed well with the world. A monthly Amway meeting had us put Ben in the care of a family member and I would only stay for the afternoon session, returning in time to get Ben settled at his normal bedtime. Unexpectedly invited to share a meal with them at my return, I accepted. Our conversation started out pleasantly enough and suddenly turned sour, when my answer to their question wasn't apparently accepted with understanding. My answer was somewhat negative and taken in defensive mode, leaving me only to defend myself against physical attack and the fierce grip of my hair, dragging me through the kitchen, with intense words being exchanged, as Ben, only 4 years old, witnessed the outburst of abuse. I repeatedly voiced that they let go of me to the point I had to myself physically force myself from the grip. Finally breaking free after a couple intense minutes, I scooped Ben up, hastily raced to the car, only to be pursued to the driveway with hostile angry threats. What should I do? I was shaken and alarmed. Never had I expected this reaction. Pulling away in the car, fear of the repercussions, tears flowing in streams and sobs. I had to think clearly of my next step as I escaped any further drama. My decision was to return for Gary, hoping to find solace. His family had been called and now their perspective skewed. Only one side of the story had been told. It felt like a crash course in learning how to handle over the top circumstances that threw me to my knees in prayer. In the aftermath I sought God for my part in that day's events and wanted to know my responsibility,

I also left it in His hand to arrange for further contact which would come in the form of a meeting with the family members pastor. I prayed for truth and justice and knew my heart was not intent on vindication. Recounting the sordid details, gaining basic understanding of our lives and circumstances, he addressed the issues with wisdom and instruction. "Forgiveness is what needs to happen in this situation. You need to forgive one another. You may not feel like forgiving, but forgiveness is not a feeling. It is a choice we make because Christ choose to forgive us. We choose forgiveness instead of unforgiveness. To walk in love, you must choose to treat one another as if nothing happened that day. You might not even say today, "I forgive you.". but today you must choose in your heart to forgive and come into agreement with Jesus. Treat one another from this day as a blessing and in the future someday you will need to express verbally that you have forgiven one another. He further instructed the family member to call the rest of the family and tell them that they have chosen to forgive me, exhorting them to do the same, thus bringing reconciliation and restoration all around.

Determined to follow his wisdom and lay a foundation for restoration, I made intentional acts of blessing toward this person, watching ever so closely, as God softened my heart to the point of actual positive emotion. Seven years went by including meals shared, gifts exchanged, regular phone calls, and conversations with substantial relational connection. I decided that the time had come to express my forgiveness as the pastor encouraged us to do. Again, I was not prepared emotionally for hearing, "You forgive me?" The sarcasm smacked hard, making light of all my effort to bless and be a blessing. Jesus command to Peter was heard in my spirit. "Forgive, if necessary, seventy times seven." Getting passed it took more effort, but forgiveness despite other actions becomes easier with maturity. Maturity helps us see now the choice to forgive is individual. The sarcasm does not take away my choice to forgive nor what God sees and knows to be in my heart. I would choose forgiveness if I want to be forgiven. This was not the last time I faced choosing forgiveness for it was the life I wanted for me and others. To be free of anger and free them from my rage.

Our culture is filled with support groups to navigate and work through painful storms of life. I rely on more mature believers for support in difficulty. A spiritual pillar, and mother in the Lord, spoke to my own anger one evening. I had called her for counsel, my problems needed to hear her wisdom and she let me vent. Hearing the depth in my anger, she instructed me as a follower of Christ, I needed to let it go. I could hear myself saying within, "What will I have if I don't have my anger?" Anger had been my companion all the years of my life, manifesting to keep people away, or let them know I would reject them with angry words to keep from the hurt of their actions. Flooding tears and gut-wrenching emotion surrounded the inner voice telling me she spoke the truth. I believed she loved me and trusted that what she said would bring me closer to intimacy with Jesus, even though I didn't know exactly what would replace my anger, I needed to continue allowing the pulling out of the entwining roots that kept me reacting with anger. Peace and relief followed as we prayed that day. It felt good to let go of something that truly was not me.

Speaking with the analogy of a continuum, God showed me truth. He wanted me to see the extremes of character so I could see myself.

Sin . . . . CHRIST LOVE

Judgement. . . . . MERCY

Pre-Christian seed. . . . . .Post Christian Seed

Just a few examples and this can be used for examination of any characteristic opposites. As people we all stand hypothetically on the line of the continuum. Place yourself there and then think about the circumstances that put you there. Where you are on the continuum effects not only you but others. You cannot effectively love others if you yourself are on the continuum closer to Sin than Christ's Love. Being closer to Love means you have allowed Christ to fill you with love. We can only give what we have received. Our choices are the reason we endure consequences good or bad. Some continuums will show us balance and others the goal. For example, Sin and Love. The goal is Love, no awareness of blatant sin but an infilling daily of living a forgiven life, reliance on the Lord, and Love so we can earnestly say we live the standard of love and treat others as we ourselves would want to be treated. For me this included revelation of needed discipline and boundaries, requiring my movement to put in place the discipline and boundaries revealed through God's word and study of healthy relationship. Sometimes only I was aware of the benefit, while leaving others behind, trusting God had both, me and them, within his care.

Anger wants justice but God in his mercy chose not to give me what I deserve but instead through the blood sacrifice of Jesus that took my place, He could now treat me as if I had never sinned and teach me to hear his voice. Grace. That is the key to understanding how it is we realistically walk in Love. Extending grace to others results in compassion and mercy which triumphs in the end. And remember this, not all of us are on the same point in our journey so some may not know grace the way you do. God will show you how to extend grace. Be willing and you will see amazing things happen in others. This example helped me in so many situations. Learning my own need for mercy transferred to all my relationships as a discipline of the Spirit. Not only did it apply to my discipline as His child, but also to my lack of discipline as my parent's child. It was crucial for the sake of my own children to see me operate in a spirit that was merciful and not extreme judgement. God had to move me toward mercy as he healed me. His mercy softened my judgements and eventually erased the need for my own form of justice. Judge not lest you be judged, held new meaning. Let the Lord judge your soul, perfecting you in His likeness. I learned revenge is the Lord's. In his time, the circumstances of life will reveal God's standard. Above all others, our submission to him, and his discipline of loving us into seeing the benefit for good, giving us standards to stabilize us even in the various trials and difficulties, life throws our way.

CHAPTER 3 🌿

Cultivating and Fertilizing

Rely on the Lord,

For only He can turn

A Mess into a Message

A Trial into a Triumph

And what's broken into something beautiful.

—Zandra Vranes

Entering each new season would test my character. The Gardener's trowel would dig deeply to weed out unseemly attitudes of my soul which had rooted themselves, to replace them with Himself and His Love and fruit of the Holy Spirit. It's a good thing that nothing is too difficult for God. Dave and Sheri, examples of Christ, shone forth in the fruitfulness of the Church's fellowship and growth, offering me stability in relationship I had not had. I was hungry and went to an additional church Sunday Evening and a women's prayer group Thursday. All of these, spurring my personal growth to new heights and depths.

Relationship is too important in the realm of life. Not wanting to continue in ways experienced growing up, change to break cycles holding me captive by heritage and ignorance, I would need the Holy Spirit to reveal and dynamite the old foundations to dislodge and destroy anything contrary to His design for me. Then my freedom and understanding would pave the way to bring others. Just like Harriet who knew in her heart God had bigger plans for her life and stepped out of her known life onto a path that would make freedom possible for a whole sector of our nation. Obedeience expands the field of our influence. The fellowship offered a way to experience freedom to worship God in new ways. Raising hands offered in surrender (even when no one else was), small group intimacy, learning scriptures, operation of spiritual gifts, supporting one another in life's seasons and fun times too, all fed the hunger I had to know God more.

Our fellowship, by example, created a worshipful atmosphere with the noticeable presence and acts of the Lord. We were beginning to sense the goodness and love of God leading us into commitment to this group. Receiving the baptism of the Holy Spirit with evidence in tongues was a gift that I would need when the battles of life seemed overwhelming.

He can turn the bad to good; as he was doing with me. People are hurting emotionally and spiritually. They are not our enemy. We must learn to see the imprint of human love verses God's love; viewing circumstances from Truth if we would know Christ. Not all true things are Truth and the difference between human perspective and God's perspective must be adjusted by the Holy Spirit's revelation of Jesus Christ and His mission to transform us into His sons and daughters. All want to be loved, needed and accepted, I would learn this from Lynn Elder speaker and author of the book I Love You but not Your Behavior. Love the sinner not the sin is the goal of the believer. The problem lies in answering that question for ourselves. We can be our own worst enemy until our spiritual vision is focused on our own sins. Christ loves me (and You) and how can I (we) live in that love and please Him. I wanted to answer that for myself. Do you? Let's do the best we can by grace to love him with as much heart, mind, body and soul and the rest it says He covers with His love. The reality of falling short is obvious to us at times and yet the reality of His forgiveness is what keeps us going for the prize as we race to win the blessings of righteous living. We start in repentance and go to the waters of baptism.

My baptisms were signs of commitment from me to covenant relationship sealed with the sacrificial blood of Christ. Jesus was first to please our father in this way and his desire is for all his children to fulfill righteousness in this way. Scripture records it this way in the AMP version. It is the beginning of lifelong relationship and how we care for that relationship is shown forth by the faith we exhibit in the Lord, whom we cannot physically see but know exists by His own faithfulness to us.

The choice of water baptism, early that first November after my conversion in 1981, was an important milestone, declaring intent to follow Christ and put off the ways of my past moving into a life of pleasing the One who gave his life for me. Our Lord was himself baptized for the fulfillment of righteousness, recorded in the Gospels of Matthew, Mark, Luke and John. Luke, the physician, describes the baptism in Chapter 3: 21-22. 21. Now when all the people had been baptized, and when Jesus also had been baptized, and [while he was still] praying, the visible heaven was opened. 22. And the voice of the Holy Spirit descended upon him in bodily form like a dove, and a voice came from heaven, saying "You are my son, My beloved! In you I am well pleased and find delight!"

Christ's blood was the sacrifice to restore mankind to his original relationship, like Adam and Eve, before great temptation, the choice they made to disobey God, convinced by the devil that they could be "as God" if only they had knowledge of good and evil. My declaration of faith in Christ's sacrifice for salvation was not going unchallenged by my enemy the devil. He wanted me to turn back and defeat me in my resolve to have new life. Water baptism was a symbolic representation of my passing from death into life. We can also enjoy the fulfillment of righteousness in obedience as we please our Father, we will find His words to ring with Truth in our spirit and put us on the path of desiring once again to choose Him above the knowledge of good and evil.

I was learning to see that God had his hand in my life even as a child, imparting good, and yet only now because of my relationship with him was I able to perceive his good influence. I was inspired to greater standards of attitude toward people and enticed to desire a large family. My desires were to live this out, imperfect as I was, relying on God's guidance and forgiveness for my weaknesses and His strength to accomplish what he could through me.

My hope to find my true God designed being was one more step closer to his likeness of me. My choice was to change me and learning to view my soul in the light gave me some indication of the process of walking to freedom by His infinite grace and mercy. The range of possibilities between two extremes; such as mercy and justice. They are extreme alone but when coupled together can be effective to bring a wise balance for relationship. My anger wanted justice but God in his mercy chose not to give me what I deserve but instead through the blood of Jesus treat me as if I had never sinned. Grace. Learning that my own need for mercy must transfer into all my relationships as a discipline of the spirit. Not only did it apply to my discipline as His child and my lack of discipline as my parent's child, but it was crucial that I learn this lesson for the sake of my own children. I had to operate in a spirit that was gentle yet firm not harsh and unbending. God has high standards for discipline, yet He loves us into seeing the benefit of discipline for good and not denial of good.

Not having had discipline of character as a child caused me to seek a mentor to learn how to discipline my children with love. The steps I learned at first were to try to work on one issue at a time and focus on that one issue until good fruit was evident. That within that context, instruction of expectation had already been taught expressly and the child had clear understanding of such expectation. Only after this was there grounds for stronger action than a reprimand. Children naturally love to please and if expectations are laid out, they know how to please you. God is like this; He lays out his desires for us and lets us choose to please Him. Secondly, have a place set apart if necessary stronger correction after defiance, is needed. Not the bedroom, but a neutral location not to disrupt the atmosphere of the rest and peace of their retreat. Thirdly, if you are feeling angry take time to chill, count, or wait until you can administer loving discipline which includes confession by the child as to the offending behavior (which they always inherently seem to know), and prayer for forgiveness and verbal acknowledgement and plea for forgiveness from anyone injured by them. It should be asking of them to express the actions they should take in the future and then any additional wisdom can be taught to help if needed. I love the statement I heard regarding disciplining children which says, you never have to teach a child to do wrong, they do that naturally, you only must teach them to do right.

I was not perfect at this and my children suffered as I learned the process. My own fears of them traveling down the same path I had often colored my actions in darker shades of gray not having yet attained to seeing my soul's darkness fully. I allowed Holy Spirit to convict me if I erred and my heart was broken at my own lack when conviction came.

I would come to know that God loves a broken and contrite heart, because it is willing and able to be molded like the clay in the potter's hands. I was desperate for his ways to bridge the gap between my life and His kingdom.

Eight years would pass, and I was growing but the struggles at time put me on my face in tears of distress and want of freedom from such. Would the struggle ever end? I was reminded often of the promise of Psalm 126: 5 KJV They who sow in tears shall reap in joy and singing. A few years before that our family would celebrate our nation's freedom with a trip to my father's log house with friends from our church. The wife had been my mentor since college days through an internship with Pennsylvanians for Human Life. Traveling a great distance, with delay in departure, I rode with her and some of the five children. I was blaming Gary for the delay and my attitude was not in line with goodness and conducive to a great start for our time together.

She tolerated me into the hours of Sunday evening during meal prep, while the guys and children were outside enjoying a campfire, she expressed her frustration, for she and her husband, their view of my appalling behavior toward Gary. I felt attacked. I had been praying to learn appropriate submission and the fire for my testing was engulfing me in inferno of anger, sending me in a tantrum to the upper level in tears. On impulse I left her to finish the dinner.

Her words of truth, no matter how harsh, had struck a tender spot of lacking character in me. She had spoken to a heart issue of disrespect; the Holy Spirit was after it and I would retreat to my old behavior that caused me to fight. Not only with her but with myself. I did not want to face the truth at that moment, but then facing the truth is not a matter of convenience. It would require time for me to get over the anger and hear God's voice, however, he did speak quickly using my dear eldest son, five years of age.

Entering the room, he asked me what was wrong. I told him that I hated myself for the way I was acting, and he should not be worried. I told him that I loved him, and he responded with wisdom beyond his years. "Mommy, you can't love me if you don't love yourself!" I was blindsided. Another flesh wound, quick and sharp, attempting to show me my errant thought, reminding me of his word in Hebrew 4:12 AMP; For the word of God speaks is alive and full of power[making it active, operative, energizing, and effective]; it is sharper than any two-edged sword, penetrating to the dividing line of the "breath of life(soul) and [the immortal] spirit, and of joints and marrow [of the deepest parts of our nature], exposing and sifting and analyzing and judging the very thought and purposes of the heart.

The night passed, and morning came with no further communication. I stayed hidden away with my cold indifferent anger and rage. The family left and shortly after we departed cutting our time away short and ruining any celebratory plans. The drive home was like a scene from "Frozen"!

I did not speak for a week. I lay in my squalor… in the house upon a bed of stubborn refusal to submit to the Truth. Then it came, His voice, again speaking Truth. "Susan, if you don't let me tell you what to do, then you cannot be my disciple". That was something to consider. Of course, He knew my heart was to be His disciple and yet He told me of my option. It was in my face, I clearly only had one choice if I wanted to follow Him.

That's how it works, He overwhelms you with love that tastes so good to your hungry heart and then you know there is no other choice but Him. To submit to Him because He will meet your deepest needs. Praise God, he knew I would choose him, and he so graciously understands our fleshly weaknesses and strongholds and knows exactly how to severe the ties. Now, I was set to walk in the grace apportioned in the blessing of submission.

Added to the foundation stone of submission would also be sowing. This lesson would help me to overcome selfish ways and build His Kingdom by faith. Giving of all that I possessed, because I saw that without him, I could do or possess nothing. I learned to observe according to the spirit the needs of people. I made it a spiritual discipline to pray with a person who ask for prayer not trusting my memory and using this to build faith in the heart of the person asking for prayer. If I ask in faith, I believed it was heard and I could rest assured that in His time and way it would be answered. I was also given to hospitality, my mother had been as well. It was enjoyable to host believers for gatherings including celebrations, dinners, campfires, picnics, small group meetings, prayer, counseling: all done for the Lord who presence was invited to saturate the atmosphere and bring joy into the lives of those I could. If there was reason to be hospitable, I gladly would be even without prior planning. Our home would also see transitional house guests come and go. Various needs of housing brought them to ministry. Separation, abuse, releases from the hospital, a guardian in the hospital, lost housing, and even hunger and abandonment. Then there were guests such as children's friends, international students needing respite and new vistas away from college life, old friends visiting and relatives.

One of our most memorable occasions came when we had a "For Sale by Owner" sign on the house. We were just sitting down to a large pot of soup, salad and warm corn bread and a knock came at our front door. Smiling faces and apologies for disruption were spoken and they ask if it would be to out of the question to view the house now as they were on their way through town and had no other time apart. I told them we had just sat down to eat and ask if they had done so. I was trusting the Lord to increase the food as he had done with the loaves and fishes and if they stayed, I was confident He would do so now. It turned out to be a most pleasant fellowship as they were believers as well and we had so much to talk about in that regard. The food never ran out! They didn't buy the house and yet our acquaintance was one of "in the moment" and brought the presence of the Lord in greater measure to our meal and home. I loved these types of encounters as they showed that God was always faithful in His provision, because we always seemed to have more than enough. An essential quality to develop is flexibility. It will always avail to wonderful opportunity of surprise encounters.

The Growing of a Rose

In the first fall of our marriage, our young adult group, lead by Dave and Sheri took us on retreat to a cabin, north of our home in the mountains. Fellowship, teaching, and lots of fun would create a deeper bond of affection among us. We were all new acquaintances as the church was growing at a rapid pace attracting many new faces. It was on this trip that we announced to them that we would have a baby in July the following year. We would be one of five couples expecting in the new year. There was much to celebrate and plenty of love all around. Hot-dog eating contests, volleyball, extreme cold dips in the creek, and our first foot washing.

Holy Spirit was always invited to lead, and this time was no different; we were being trained to hear his voice and act accordingly. Forming a circle of worship with a chair, basin and towel in the center, we waited until someone heard the name of the person to whom Christ wanted to minister through them. Then they approached the basin and ministered; some prayers, words of knowledge, words of encouragement etc. Christ had given the example and it is a humbling experience to both give and receive of another's service. A gesture of honor and hospitality offered to guests in His culture, often including the placement of a laurel wreath upon the head for honor: to wash away the dust on the feet from a dusty road traveled. John 13 records Peter refusing Christ's desire to wash his feet and Christ's reply was "Unless I wash you, you have no part of Me. In other words, no companionship. He wanted them to understand what He was doing and in verse 14 AMP it says "If I then your Lord and Teacher (Master) have washed your feet, you ought [it is your duty., you are under obligation, you owe it] to wash one another's feet.

I was not unacquainted with voices whispering words of "put down" and would hear such as I waited to express that "nobody loves you and no-one is going to wash your feet"! It was time to speak Truth to the lies. I would not be swayed to believe I was not loved. Someone may not wash my feet, but Jesus loves me and that was fact. Settled in my heart and not negotiable. I was indeed the last one to be called and had to battle until the moment my name was called. Dave's voice had spoken it, letting me know I was not forgotten. Feeling much like I imagine the woman at the well, I knew his call meant Christ's love affirming my acceptance and forgiveness. In the past prostituting myself to the whims of my emotions momentarily was what I did; but now Christ was letting me know that my emotions were not the issue of control but my belief and spoken Word were what kept me in His care. Dave was His chosen vessel and he revealed even more of our story; telling that in high school he would lay hands on my locker and speak "God, you go get that wild woman!" This honor was humbling and would fill my soul with goodness that increased my faith to new heights and depths.

So happy was I. However, my next testing of faith would not be a far off. Thanksgiving and Christmas approached and for the weeks before I rallied in our cabin weekend and all it had accomplished, but word was spreading through Gary's work of imminent layoffs of massive proportion with the Bethlehem Steel Corporation. We wondered if his twelve years of employment would be enough to buffer and protect us. They were in fact not enough as notice was received the week after Christmas; which sent my anxiety souring. With a new baby coming there would be needs and I was so used to having everything provided; not ever having known want.

Along with the notice, came depression upon Gary's soul. He had unrealistically thought he would work there the rest of his life and upon retirement receive a sizable pension. The future looked grim for the company and a permanent closure loomed in the possible near months. Unemployment Compensation was available and in Gary's thought, enough to see us through. His lack of motivation to seek employment elsewhere combined with the lack of help at home, while I went to school and took care of the house and Ben, made me frustrated.

It was only earlier in the fall that I was finding dissatisfaction in my business curriculum and prayed to see if there should be changes made to another major. Options included staying in my current major, changing majors and or changing schools, possibly a bible school. My answer had come, and it was to remain at the same school but change my major to Social Service. In addition, I had clearly understood God to speak the words "I cannot teach you to be a woman in a man's dominated world." It made sense as my counselor had told me that I thought and reasoned like a man. Obviously growing up with my father and three brothers and a whole host of male friends in our neighborhood had clear influence.

I liked the field of Social Work for the fact it was a people focused field. The philosophy of it however revealed conflict with the biblical viewpoint and I would come to recognize that my Marxist/Socialist professors hoped to indoctrinate the future generation with these views of a society which believe the means of production, distribution and exchange should be owned or regulated as a whole, a transitional social state somewhere between the over-throw of capitalism and the realization of communism. Concepts sounded much like the biblical teaching of Christ; including brotherhood, community, fellowship and unity. However, the means to the end was law: not love. Lies not Truth. Communities of this philosophy had failed miserably around the world; and one in the US lead by the Shakers and Josiah Warren around the beginning of the 19th century. The Shaker experiment had failed to reproduce its own kind and today only two members remain according to Wikipedia recording on the last Shaker Village now on US soil in Maine. The Josiah Warren village in New Harmony Indiana only lasted two years in the 1800's.

At first my attention was drawn in by these similar concepts, but I wanted to be sure that this was indeed what it seemed to be and ask the Lord to show me His perspective. I came to understand that to make lies subtler they only need to be mixed with a little Truth. The deception is easier that way because it requires the listener who is hearing to seek further for themselves as to the foundations. Most will not seek further as it is our nature to believe those teaching have the answers. We usually don't question and so as not to be blatant the mix of truth with a lie makes it hardly noticeable to the undiscerning mind and heart.

An aunt of mine, also a believer, told me that if I only ever ask for one gift of the Lord it should be that I ask for discernment; enabling me to see clearly the Truth from a lie; good from evil. No good is good if it is not based in Truth and motivated by the Father. Jesus said himself He can do nothing except His Father tell him. Adam and Eve ate from the tree of the knowledge of good and evil and they were cast from the garden of Eden with it. The tree of Life is the only tree to produce authentic Good through the Life-giving spirit of the Father who was made manifest in Christ Jesus. Genesis in the Bible tells the whole story and John 4:24 AMP state God is a spirit and those who worship Him must worship Him in spirit and in truth (reality). It would be this knowledge that motivated me to pray before my classes for questions to be given to me that would expose the deceptions in the theory. Without fail, God would answer my prayer and the frustration seen in my professor as he tried to avoid calling on me and his anger was evident by the red color which rose each time up his neck and onto his face. He could not avoid my questions, making him to look ignorant if he did so. So, I would ask, and he would stumble for an answer. It became obvious his foundations of theory were shaky at best. I was a few years of age ahead of my fellow classmates. They voiced appreciation of my input into the class discussions, saying along with it that it caused them to look with different perspective.

Concurrently in the new year of 1983 we had committed to attend with the church a Marriage Encounter weekend retreat at a local center with a group of about fifty-six. The honeymoon was over. Real life was dictating a need for help to keep our marriage from failure. The opening session Friday evening included introductions with analogy of spouses. Seated halfway around the large semi-circle we both had time to pray and think upon our analogy. I needed help to see through the fog covering my mind and heart to see Gary's potential and likeness to God. God spoke. "A young oak tree who would grow to spread its branches over our family; planted by streams of living water, providing shelter and protection for us." I shared first and then Gary. "My wife reminds me of a rose." Sighs arose around the room from the women. "She is beautiful to look at, but you have to watch out how you handle her, or you might get pricked!" My face flushed as loud laughter erupted throughout the room. Somewhat thrilled and otherwise embarrassed, my conflicting emotions would have to be contemplated. What did all this analogy hold for revelation of the woman I was now and the one I was to become in the future?

Saturday's sessions of teaching and written intimate communications proved to be challenging. I was wanting Gary to express the truth in hope of opening our relationship to deeper understanding and more effective problem solving. However, my emotional state of stress was off the chart, hormones of pregnancy, lay-offs, learning to trust God, and difficulty maneuvering the marriage path. I did find God to be there and speaking to our life and I was hopeful of a successful outcome to the efforts.

The evening session would eventually end with elements given to share intimate communion with Christ in our private rooms. Before this we were asked to examine our heart for any offences against our spouse and then willingly ask and receive forgiveness. Quietly, introspection became the posture to achieve this and then we were to proceed to the table with the elements. I bowed my head and ask for any unconfessed sin against Gary to be revealed. I heard nothing and opened my eyes. Gary proceeded to confess and ask my forgiveness, and I then gave it. I remained quiet and within moments Gary said in a judgmental tone, "What about YOU!?" My anger was roused. Why would I confess something I didn't hear? How dare he question my ability to hear in the quiet and surrender which pervaded the atmosphere of the time. I was not moving to the table and I was not taking communion with someone who distrusted me. Time passed as all other participants

moved out and I was forced to save face (a mistake) to move
as well. Picking up the elements we were greeted farewells and
handed a single red rose. Ugh! I felt vulnerable and caught by my
father in an immature fit of angry emotion and faced with the very
real likeness of His vision of beauty expressed only a night ago by
my husband. Little did we expect the events of the night to follow.

The torrent of emotions let loose within moments of shutting
the door behind us, even getting physical. My only solution was
to remove myself to calm and reflect and express my state to
the Lord, a railroad tie in the parking lot would suffice for the
attitude adjustment. Releasing all the emotion allowed for the
eventual ability to hear His voice showing me my responsibility
to make amends with Gary which meant returning to the room.
I approached with desire to obey and hopeful we could move on
in peace. However, Gary had not yet the same desire and I was
met with more of his sarcasm and hurtful words, causing my
immediate return to anger and tossing of my communion wine
into his face. Gary was on his way to the bathroom to clean up and
I grabbed the keys to the car and was going home. There seemed
no reason to stay. The impasse too great for me and my immature
ways. Thoughts of someone calling me to encourage my return
crossed my mind frequently as I drove the thirty minutes to home.
It would be 11:30 pm as I pulled in the driveway. No one called,
and I went to bed.

It was sometime after I had fallen asleep, I was awakened. It
was the Lord Himself who came to get me. "Get up now, enough
of this, I want you to repent and return to the camp." My cocky
arrogance quickly showed itself in reply. "If you want me to repent,
you will have to make me!" If there ever was a time for the ever-

imagined lightening to strike me down, it would have been then. No, it didn't happen, but five minutes later without further words only his presence, I was exiting my bed, tears in my eyes, headed for my knees to hit the floor in front of my favorite chair, crying in revelation of His love for a prodigal who desperately needed love to change her heart. He knows the hidden desire of our heart and when it is completely set on His purpose for life. No one knows it with clarity until it is made real in experience.

Repentance complete, I wanted to take a shower before returning. It was now 3:30 am and Gary would be sleeping. I should have time for a shower. Asking Him if it was okay, but he knows the thoughts and intentions of our heart and he spoke again: "No shower, go now." "Please?", I entreated. "No, I want you to leave without." No more argument I grabbed my coat and keys and jumped in the car stopping only momentarily to pick up mail for the day at the mailbox. Among the mail there was a personal handwritten envelope which I could not wait to open. The contents revealed a cashier's check in the amount of a bill we owed that no one, but the Lord, could possibly have known. Whoever was the benefactor had listened to God, and His grace was evident. I certainly did not deserve such a blessing after the way I had behaved, But God…

It was now shortly passed the 4 am hour and arriving back at the retreat it was as I suspected; Gary was asleep, and I would have to waken him with banging on the window to come and open the door. Both of us softened in disposition by the events; spent the next couple hours before breakfast reconciling our relationship. I truly wanted a God filled marriage and would continue to follow His leading to make it happen.

God's hand in planning this weekend was very evident and it felt as if it was all and only for us. I know that isn't true, but it felt that way. The sessions following would only emphasize it more as the day went on with more "coincidences". I believe nothing is coincidence and asking the Lord to be involved in our life emphasizes this fact as He reveals to our eyes, ears and heart the connections of circumstance to work out his plans.

As the day passed and our time at the retreat nearing an end, our leaders, Jerry and Mary Ann (our prior spouses same names), ask for testimonials of God's work in the couples' hearts from the sessions. Healing, restoration, renewal, all these were spoken and then I shared from the beginning to the end all that God had done. A hush fell and hearts of joy, and tears of gladness were expressed at the details of God's love toward us and a vocal appreciation for our willingness to open our lives to scrutiny. Bill and Mary approached at the close with tears in Bill's eyes, he began to share his own story that related to ours. He had a dream three weeks before this weekend which he didn't understand or have revelation about but knew it was a dream from God. Only as I shared did it become clear that he saw the weekend we just experienced. In the dream, He and Mary were in a place with about the same number of couples. It was night and one of the couples had a horrific fight and the wife left the place in a huff, however she returned by 4 am the next morning. By this time in his story I had a realization and tears were pouring forth from my eyes. A struggle in knowing I was loved was now being transformed by the fact that God had shown Bill my ugly actions and the events of the previous night to bring me assurance of His love and acceptance even when I was unlovely and acting out of hurt and woundedness. My past was one of rejection and rejecting, to protect myself, but my New Love, in His sovereign ability, let me know most assuredly that His Love would be with me when I was not even loving toward others or Him. I would learn to repent and change my minds thoughts and my hearts actions to please this One who gave me hope and life with a future of goodness. My hope is that you too will know that no matter what you have done or what has been done to you, that God's arm is not too short or his love unable to transform your life when you truly desire a relationship of trust with Him. I am living proof of how His loving kindness and truth can turn a broken wounded soul into a whole being with a grateful, giving love. I want His love and discipline.

The likeness of the words discipline, and disciple are purposeful and intentional. In becoming a disciple, life becomes clear in purpose and intention. With the discipline of the Lord's ways we get to this place. We learn the purpose of the word in Romans 8:28-implication of why "all things work together for good". It reads in the Amplified version:

28. We are assured and know that [God being a partner in their labor] all things work together and are [fitting into a plan] for good to and for those who love God and are called according to [His] design and purpose. 29. For those whom he foreknew [of whom He was aware and loved beforehand]. He also destined from the beginning [foreordaining them] to be molded into the image of His Son [and share inwardly His likeness]. That He might become the firstborn among many brethren.

The Message defines the cost of discipleship. Luke 14:26 says it like this:

One day when large groups of people were walking along with him, Jesus turned and told them, "Anyone who comes to me but refuses to let go of father, mother, spouse, children, brothers, sisters-yes even oneself! cannot be my disciple.

By the time I heard about having a personal relationship with Christ, I was ready to follow Him. It would take him years of training and discipline to get me to the place of freedom and good choices, traveling the road of life was difficult and emotional but my choice to follow would continue to remain firm, because I know the benefit to my mind, will and emotions. Oswald Chambers in his devotional "My Utmost for His Highest", writes on March 12, "When we come up against the barriers of natural relationship, where is Jesus Christ? Most of us desert Him- "Yes Lord, I did hear They call, but my mother is in the road, my wife, my self interest and I can go no further." Continuing his explanation Oswald further says, "The test of abandonment is always over the neck of natural devotion Go over it and God's own abandonment will embrace all those you had to hurt in abandoning. Beware of stopping short of abandonment to God. Most of us know abandonment in vision only." My prayer was to be totally abandoned to God.

Declaring this as a truth I wanted to live and acting toward such a life, my favorite life verse became Isaiah 50:7 AMP For, the Lord God helps me; therefore, Have I not been ashamed or confounded. Therefore, have I set My face like a flint and know that I shall not be put to shame. Writing it down on 3x5 notecards and placing it on my bathroom mirror and kitchen window, I reminded my self until I was living the truth of it and repeated its life-giving words whenever needed during hard times. Seeking

God's help in all circumstances, I trusted His words to annihilate humiliation and shame along the path of my journey toward becoming like Him. To which end I would enter the Kingdom by grace and mercy, obtaining fulfillment of my being and purpose as His daughter and bride.

In all my learning I had to set goals of achievement to lead me on a corrected course. Firstly, defining my role as a Christian woman. Secondly, develop conviction by the Word and my actions. Thirdly, Become quiet, vocally, mentally, and spiritually. Fourthly, discover and develop my calling and the gifts which would enhance that calling. And lastly, in all these things find acceptance in the becoming.

That spring would bring the rains of the Holy Spirit through the musical production, The Witness, directed by Sheri Hess and performed by our young adult group during Easter and months following as we took the show on the road to local churches, spreading the good news of Christ and His resurrection. Energized and invigorated our faith was pushed to new heights and depths as we publicly proclaimed hope with joy so others could see and receive the Lord and have relationship as well. We bonded in group and as couples and friends.

We had already welcomed some of the five babes expected, July was approaching fast. Ours was coming in the heat of summer with sweltering humidity, approximately due July 9th. I was huge from my perspective and I do not fair well in heat so when that day came and went, I needed encouragement to endure. To get my thoughts off the waiting, Mom and Dad thought a round of pitch and putt would do the trick and possibly speed up the process. After which we enjoyed dinner at the Historical Lincoln House where Lincoln himself had dined. It had the desired effect and to our delight labor began in the evening hours the following day and 6 and 1/2 hours later our son, Nathan Ericus was ecstatically welcomed into the family. A beautiful gift and joyfully received by his big brother Ben, who thanked us repeatedly and wanted to hold him right away.

Two days passed as we returned and settled into home. We were so happy to have Nathan but only two days into our routine he began running a fever, with little desire to a nurse. My concern was heightened and a call to our family physician assured me it was most likely nothing to worry about. Baby aspirin and continued watch should take care of it in a couple of days. If not, then a call back would be in order. He didn't improve and in fact grew lethargic, causing me angst and the need for the second call. Answered with an apparent disregard to his state and mine, the doctor didn't even want to see him. I called Mom. She an R.N. would certainly give me some wisdom; however, I did have some fear about her faith in the doctor expecting her to say trust his judgement. On the contrary, she encouraged a second opinion bringing relief from fear and a call was quickly made to our birth pediatrician. Friends were visiting when all this happened and were sensitive to my concern, offering to drive us. I was feeling overwhelmed with emotion and noticed the thoroughness of the examination. There was definite concern on the doctor's face and with all seriousness he said that he wanted to admit him to the hospital for testing. He said I could go immediately or wait until morning. "If it were you, what would you do?", I asked. His reply quick and definitive, "I would not wait." Phone calls for the admission were made and we left, in a whirl of worry and tears.

I was overwhelmed by fear. Gary was called and would meet us there and prayers were spoken and requested for all that faced us in this time.

After admission I found out Nathan's first test was to be a spinal tap. Watching with empathic pained helplessness on the other side of the windowed door. My heart cried out to God. "Please save my baby!", as tears and great sobs of distress poured forth from my being.

Chapter 4 🌿

Beauty and the Beast

"All the world is full of suffering-it is also full of overcoming."
—Helen Keller

…After what seemed like hours, Nathan was placed in a room, hooked up to monitors and IV. Beside him as he tried to rest, on a floormat, a battle of darkness and light, would make itself known, trying to overcome and defeat me in my state of emotional vulnerability. My thoughts and heart in turmoil were searching for peace and wisdom for my child's wellness when interrupted. A voice spoke. "Your baby is going to die." I knew that voice. It wasn't my Lord. Roused and awakened, I was not going to agree with that statement because I knew it was not the will of my Father that this child who was set apart and sanctified by my own free will by prior agreement to God's purposes, should be taken. It was time to fight!! I drew my spiritual sword and thrust truth at the enemy's lie. "No! He isn't devil, you can't have him. He was set apart and sanctified to God's kingdom even while still in my womb. You need to shut your lying mouth. God is going to heal him!" My shield of faith was up for protection and the thrust effective. Trusting and knowing by faith, God was with me in this trial and test, I called Sonia in the morning. Relaying the past day's events, I entreated her to pray. Her response was immediate availability. Without hesitation, she dropped her plans and brought her husband to the hospital for support.

"The doctor is not the last word, God is", she stated boldly. "May I hold him?" Gathering our babe with all his attachments into her loving arms she and I sat, together, our husbands knelt before us. Peter began praying and Sonia says nothing is going through to heaven, we need rhema (current word from the Lord). Continuing in agreement by faith, some time passed; Sonia suddenly exclaimed with confidence "No need to worry, baby healed. I feel power of God go through me to baby. Baby healed!!" Gary confirmed that he too had felt power during those moments. Tears of joy followed by hugs of love, believing God had indeed brought healing and victory for this battle.

Evidence came forth immediately as his countenance, color, and appetite was restored and his fever dissipated with completeness by the next morning. Skulking in the shadows, the enemy continued trying to steal our joy and of course our testimony. Clearly the doctors and staff knew something unexplainable happened. Nathan was no longer sick. We knew what had taken place and could explain it in spiritual terms, but their quandary kept them looking for answers in the natural realm, along with their skepticism of the supernatural power of God. Unnecessary tests continued for days, leaving Nathan with a scar on his left hand when enhancing ink, used for a cat scan blew out and onto his skin creating a hole, the scar of the hole remains on his hand and he is now a man. Nate's scar reminds me of the scars on Christ's nail scarred hands and always of God's goodness in healing Nathan. I was grateful, after 10 long days, we could return to our home and family. The battle won but the war was still on.

Warrior, Intercessor, Overcomer! Before I knew Christ, an awareness of a dark world invaded my life through dabbling with things I thought were innocent fun. Ouija Board, levitation, seances and pow-wow were experimented. At times I have gone back to watch movies and shows I liked as a child, determining their influence. Just recently was watching "I Love Lucy" and was totally taken back, aware that even on a show thought of as wholesome, there was a séance portrayed. I learned just enough for danger to await opportunity. Armed with this little knowledge a door opened. Pajama parties were often full of opportunities to participate in games of all kinds, among unsuspecting, unsupervised very young children becoming young adults. Most of which were unlikely to produce good fun. Unlike our youth when witchcraft was less obvious and not so acceptable, today's youth and parents think nothing of portrayals of witchcraft. Yet God has told us to have nothing to do with them. Leviticus 19: 31, the Message version speaks Gods will, "Don't dabble in the occult or traffic with mediums; you'll pollute you souls. I am God, Your God."

One night, in my early teens, I was asked to lead a séance. Following what I could only have known through outside influences we used this knowledge to begin. Setting the scene, we invited dark supernatural manifestations to intervene and co-intersect with our atmosphere. One girl was overcome, speaking in a voice not her own. Other signs brought great fear of entering into a realm we didn't know how to navigate, and we quickly ended.

Frantic emotion enveloped the room, as turning on the lights revealed a huge hole in the wall of the room.

Asking around if anyone had gone through the wall during the hubbub, we determined that it must have been put there by supernatural forces. Scared and sure, I had dabbled in a realm we should leave alone. Supernatural manifestations happened way past that night, because we had invited dark spirits to come. I was ignorant of understanding future consequences even though I chose that day to never participate again in that activity.

However, the permission granted had not been revoked spiritually, only naturally. Slyly, the devil gained access in a greater measure to my soul. By the time this realization came to pass, awareness of his assault came after giving my life to Christ, who graciously gave light to shine in the darkness of my past. The Beast was lurking about my atmosphere, enabled by my choices to take ground, but with the light of Christ shining, a beautiful rose could come forth.

Mighty transformation, through intervention and learning, exposed darkness. Submitting to fight in the war for Life with the Lord Jesus by his Holy Spirit was the necessary ingredient for beauty. His ways are not our ways and His thoughts are not ours. Isaiah 55:8. For My thoughts are not you thought neither are your ways my ways, says the Lord. 9. For as the heavens are higher than the earth, so are My ways higher than your ways and My thoughts than your thoughts. Is 55:8-9 AMP The process of submission to love Him with my whole being, heart, mind and strength would require many choices yet unfamiliar to my old nature, but on the journey, choices evolve to the point of no longer struggling. The nature of Christ becomes your new nature. A continuum with old nature on one end and new on the other.

Using the example of sowing seeds. Dark or Light seeds, sowing and reaping through life. Until we know Him, we sow in darkness. At the point we begin to understand His will for us in sowing, we will soon start sowing these seeds of life. However, spiritual and natural laws dictate that if we plant corn seeds, we reap corn, and if we plant dark sinful seed, we reap dark sinful consequences. Darkness gives way to light when turned on naturally and the same law applies spiritually. Light increased will push away the darkness. The more Christ, who is the light of the world, shines in our spirit and soul, giving way to good deeds (seeds of light), the more light we reap to push out the darkness within, bringing with it an understanding of who He is and His desires for us and the world. All His desires for us are good. Believing God is good and doing what he commands will get you to His plans and destiny for your life. Remain focused on relationship with Him by way of submission.

Submission is a dirty word for most, because our sinful nature does not like to be told what to do. It was to me. I thought it was like being negatively controlled. A submissive character is far from negative and the values of today's culture. Yet it is the very quality that promotes respect and growth. Authority is not totalitarian but allows free choice within the will of God's Kingly government. Some things such as Gods word are absolute, but whether you want to drink your coffee black or with creamer is not. Personally, I like mine black. Learning where he gives freedom depends a lot on his call in your life. Who does he want you to reach with the good news? He wants us to freely obey his precepts because we understand and know his good and omniscient (All-knowing) character. Yet he gives us freedom even to choose life or death.

A natural illustration of this is found in product manufacture. Whoever created a product knows the product best and how it works. God know how he created us and how to avoid decision based in sinful, lustful flesh. The three roots of sin are the lust of the flesh, the lust of the eyes, and the pride of life [1 John 2:16]. Adam and Eve lived out of the spirit but with boundaries before their fall from grace. I am sure that God had provided many choices for food, yet they just could not resist an apple, because they thought it was a need to have item that would make them like God! An apple that had the power to make them like God. Didn't God create them in His image?

The tree of the knowledge of good and evil was a test and they failed to trust that God would provide their needs. They chose to go beyond the boundaries in disrespect for their creator's plan and stopped growth of uninterrupted relationship with Him in the protected realm he created. They hid. They saw themselves in a bad way. I saw my own disrespect of God's boundaries and had convinced myself it wasn't that bad, using manipulative ability fooled myself and people by outward appearance. But…God is not fooled. Galatians 6:7 will confirm this fact.

Submitting myself in fullness, to principles of discipline, would keep my heart, mind, will and emotions from destructive ways. I had been given the choice to freely decide on how much or how little I wanted His life gift. Yielding to Him as the Master of the Universe, undertaking to have a relationship, was made possible by His sacrifice. My beginning was to cooperate with Him in digging up the problem seeds I had freely chosen to sow previously. Studying the Bible, combined with taking steps in obedience brought restoration and newness to all the areas of my life. I Corinthians 6:14-19 Amp says "And God both raised the Lord to life and will also raise us up by His power. Do you not see and know that your bodies are members (bodily parts) of Christ (the Messiah)? Am I therefore to take the parts of Christ and make [them] parts of a prostitute? Never! Never! Or do you not know and realize that when a man joins himself to a prostitute, he become one body with her? The two, it is written, shall be come one flesh. [Gen. 2:24] But the person who is united to the Lord becomes one spirit with Him. Shun immorality and all sexual looseness [flee from impurity in thought, word, or deed]. Any other sin which a man commits is one outside the body but he who commits sexual immorality sins against his own body. Do you not know that your body is the temple (the very sanctuary) of the Holy Spirit Who lives within you, Whom you have received [as a Gift] from God? You are not your own. You were bought with a price [purchased with a preciousness and paid for, made His own]. So then, honor God and bring glory to Him in your body.

I Kings records the reign of Solomon who built a temple for Hebrew worship of the Lord. It was his crowning achievement as the wisest human king to that point. The temple held many symbolic objects, the most important being The Ark of the Covenant, a symbol of God's presence with the people, holding the tablets of the Ten Commandments, given to Moses after the children of Israel were freed from bondage in Egypt. Built in the capital city of Israel, Jerusalem was the setting in 960 B.C. (before Christ's birth). I Chronicles 28 holds the history of it's building for all time. For my reference though, I want readers to know the temple was glorious and the word of God and His presence resided, resting within its walls. A pre-resurrection type and picture of the New Covenant when the Holy Spirit of God would bring glory and rest to Jesus within the body of believers through Christ's indwelling our bodily temple. This is still His will in the new covenant bought and sealed with Christ's blood and resurrection from the dead. He desires us to be a living temple of His word and presence.

At this point I neither felt glorious or rested even though I was seeking Him and His presence in me daily. The good seed planting stages of the growth process were moving forward with preparations to make me as beautiful as any rose. The rose I think best exhibits this process is the Joseph's Coat, one my husband gifted me on our anniversary. The new buds appear red like the blood of Christ. Within days the petals change color to orange and unfold to reveal the color blend of red and yellow. Yellow representing light. The light of Christ infiltrating our temple pushing away the darkness giving way to total yellow, then turning pink. A blend of red and white. Always the hint of red is there reminding us that it is the blood that cleanses. Finally, the flower turns white, pure and clean and beautiful in its glory. God's truth revealed in nature making us amazed and aware of the complexity of creation. My next battle to make me amazed and aware was just around the turn…

Celebrating my brother's marriage in the weeks following and enjoying our victory the rest of the summer, fall arrived as usual. Jan needed a place to stay so we opened our doors for her to become a part of the family. It was good to have her there as a friend to all. Supporting us through Nathan's illness, we now could support her when she needed us. She and I would talk at length about our lives and often on the kitchen floor in the evenings when the children were tucked in and things were quiet. One conversation has never left my memory, well at least part of it. Showing an ungodly attitude in my words, she told me to stop acting like a snot brat. Hitting the mark with her rebuke, made me consider and repent of my bad attitude, bringing appreciation to our friendship. She cared enough to speak firm truth, not allowing fear of repercussion in that moment.

That experience was only one of many with people who dared to point me in the right direction of thinking and acting. It is so important when trying to grow that we allow, not only friends, but others to lead us to Christ. What I am trying to say is sometimes we will be offended by what someone says to us, about us, but the habit of considerate listening will cause us to grow as we take what was said to Jesus in prayer. Ask Him if what they said was true and wait for His answer. Sometimes we may have to pray more than once but if we seriously want to know then He will answer. If the answer is "yes", then it is time to change your mind (repent) and learn the words of God that pertain to having that specific godly attitude. On the other side of the spectrum, when we know that our actions and attitudes have changed, we can approach Him, assured the answer we hear will be "No". Then we must remain steadfast in the fact that we know He always sees us correctly in the light of His truth. In these times my favorite quote to myself; "What you think of me is none of my business" followed by "but what God thinks of me is all that matters!"

Nathan would soon enough be eight months old and we would again be pregnant with another child due in December of 1984.

Of course, like most who choose to have multiple children above the number of two we would be asked many times, "Do you know what's causing this?" Or "You are having another?" or my favorite was those who would say sarcastically, "God Bless you!" to which my reply was "He already has!" In the duration, I would complete my Senior College Seminar working with disabled children in a United Cerebral Palsy pre-school, learning compassion for the children and parents and also recognizing the harsh reality of people in the workforce who had none. I was shocked that they thought that they could speak negatively in front of the pupil and presume they didn't hear. I was dismayed by adults who were to care for these children and didn't by action show it. I wanted to be different and spoke up, to my detriment but nevertheless for my own growth in standing for righteous action. Time spent in prayer for children, parents and teachers alike eased painful observations and yet heartfelt compassion for those who could not speak for themselves stirred my soul. Proverbs 31: 8 exhorts us "Speak up for those who cannot speak for themselves." All the while I am learning to accept others, I predominately struggle with self-rejection. Wanting to change this Luke 10:27, Proverbs 23:12 and John 13:16-17 would help me gain new knowledge and ammunition to combat my old thoughts and renew my mind to be the new me. Making God's word part of us makes us able to become and remind ourselves how to please our Father in heaven. He created us and what he says about us and how we are to be will ultimately strengthen us against harm.

Along with our unique design, (Psalm 139, Ephesians 1, Psalm 40, Romans 12, and I Corinthians 12) the scriptures tell us that God makes no mistakes (Eph. 1:4 and 4:12-14) and Philippians

1:6 tells us He will complete the good work He began in us. Our responsibility in this is stated in Colossians 3 which clearly tells us to put to death ad deprive the evil longing of your earthly body. Yes, we will fall, but God makes a way for us to get back up and move on toward maturity if we do. I John explains it: and if we continue to take step by step in faith, always humbly asking for help, He is faithful to be there for us. He is made perfect (in the acknowledgement of) our weaknesses and forgives every time until we have realized the putting to death of the old self.

True repentance is seeing our wrongs and changing our ways; not confessing sins and going on our way with no intention of pleasing our Father. Christ is in control when our trust is in His words and His sacrifice on the cross having made the way for us to follow Him into "Thy Kingdom come, Thy will be done on earth as it is in heaven: This Kingdom is the ultimate manifestation of Life on Earth. God's Kingdom!!!!

It took my own humbling experience to realize the world, I knew from birth, had nothing to offer in the way of permanent satisfaction. You may know the song from the 60's by Mick Jagger which resound that truth; "I Can't Get No Satisfaction". Drugs, alcohol, sexual impurity, material wealth; none of it gave me satisfaction. I didn't trust myself or anyone when starting my search for answers, to my thought, "there has to be more to life than this." Trust doesn't have to understand everything. Just know that you can trust the character of Almighty God. An example in the natural; children who trust parents. The child does not understand the parent but trusts them just the same as if they know the parent wants good for the child. Sadly, humans aren't perfect and do not know good apart from a relationship with

God. Hurt parents…Hurt Children. God states he will perfect us in Love. Character in God and His character, in his people, lets you know they can be trusted. You will know them by their fruit. Rotten Apple…Rotten fruit! Good Apple…Good fruit. God is perfect and so is His word, which works powerfully to produce good fruit in His children.

Reading the word from the King James Version of the Bible as a new believer can be hard to decipher because of its Old English language. For me it wasn't so hard because I had an English teacher that required reading Shakespeare and other Old English authors in my Senior year of high school and English was one of my best subjects. Eventually after wearing out that one, I switched to NIV, or New International Version, a more current American English version. And in conjunction I read the Living Bible, a paraphrase version written more like a book, the Revised Standard Version, the New King James Version and in 1997 Micki and Tracy, two young women I was discipling, gave me the Amplified Version which I love. Studying with different versions gives a broadened perspective and maybe one will speak to you louder. I learned, while taking graduate classes in Biblical Studies, how to use a Strong's concordance that has all the words in the KJV bible and the original language of Hebrew for the Old Testament and Greek for the New Testament and their respective meanings. I recommend learning how to use one because the scriptures became full of new meaning and excitement as I could look more deeply into them.

In reading I came across Matt 9:16 KJV "No one putteth a piece of new cloth unto an old garment, for that which is put into fill it up taketh from the garment and the rent is made worse.

Same verse in Amplified (AMP) version: And no one puts a piece of cloth that has not been shrunk on an old garment, for such a patch tears away from the garment and a worse rent (tear) is made. Now the Living Bible (TLB), "And who would patch an old garment with unshrunk cloth? For the patch would tear way and make the hole worse. As a seamstress trained from age nine this verse piqued my interest and I wanted to know the implications spiritually. Praying I ask God to show me. When on a search for an answer I would often talk to other believers, continue looking in other sources, and most of all keep asking until I got my answer. My understanding was that we just can't on our own effort make lasting changes to ourselves. We need God to do it, just like a garment can't repair a tear itself but needs a seamstress and like the patch we need to be washed and put into a place of shrunkeness; a more realistic view of ourselves, humility. God is the seamstress and humbles us so he can "fix the tear", between us and Himself. If He does the work, it will last.

Obedience is another dirty word to most, but to obey only means that we trust that the one we are obeying is asking us to do something for our good. Often for our growth, safety and protection, keeping us from harm. I grew up without spiritual discipline, but I knew a there would be consequences if I broke the house rules. My emotions were what I relied upon to make choices and they were fickle. Manipulating to get what I wanted as I grew older and was able to maneuver through situations emotionally. I was unable to realize good relationships, which as an adult I longed for in my heart. Superficial is the word to describe my relationships. Surface reveal only, and certainly not exposing any true emotional stability. Christ gave me the opportunity to have close friends. Fear of rejection ruled temporarily but when I was able to perceive its effects, I was then free to choose different actions which were connected to responding in love, not reacting in emotion. God accepted me. My strong desire for close friends pushed me to "be too much to handle". Co-dependency and neediness turned people off until balanced Interdependence on God filled the neediness. One pastor on a positive note told me my freedom to be open and vulnerable was an offence to those people who are not free. Time was a factor in overcoming rejection since it was deeply imbedded into my soul. But obedience to God became the framework for security of loving discipline.

There are over 123 verses in the Bible referring to obedience. The definition of obedience summarized on the website, basicsofthebible.org/psalm119, says it this way; "Psalm 119 is telling us that to know the Creator God you must know his law ordinance, word commandments, statutes, precepts, decrees, testimonies, way and faithfulness. This definitely takes time and as the Lord just spoke to me "Susan, everyone is on their own path in the process of knowing me. Be kind to yourself." I did not always realize how hard I was on myself.

My revelation of the spirit of rejection working in me came with the answer to the garment verse when I was talking with a friend about Jeremiah 2:13-14 AMP 13. For my people have committed two evils: They have forsaken Me, the fountain of living waters, and they have hewn for themselves cisterns, broken cisterns which cannot hold water. 14. Is Israel a servant? Is he a homeborn slave? Why has he become a captive and a prey?

The very next day God used those verses as a springboard to open my understanding of Luke 5:36-37. When we come to

Christ, we must allow the digging up of the "weeds" and "roots of weeds", baggage of the past (old wine and old garment), so that as the Living Water (new wine of God's word) is poured into us we will be able to hold onto it and have freedom and victory. Pain is involved. As Hebrews 12:19 TLB Being punished isn't enjoyable while it is happening- it hurts! But afterwards we can see the result, a quiet growth in grace and character. And more came the following day. Rejection is the root cause of my emotional anger. My moodiness is related to feeling rejected. Without digging up the roots we cannot have understanding and change in our heart because we are held in bondage to the rejection, which keeps us reacting with same trained response. More anger is connected to unmet expectations. I had come to believe if I didn't have expectations then I could not be hurt. That is a lie. We do have expectations and if we do not acknowledge them, it births another lie: which is lying to ourselves and others, since we fail to communicate our heart fully and in turn cannot come to some agreement about those expectations, which would satisfy all parties, fulfilling our need for healthy relationship.

Therefore, it has been my experience that as we follow the wisdom of Psalm 119, trusting and obeying the Lord's ways, His faithfulness will be evident in our circumstances. It covers the range of life's events and as I have said the pain of the past is a constant until we deal with it by allowing the pain of discipline which is momentary."

Fighting my spiritual enemies would require such an obedience if I were ever going to prove that I no longer wanted what they were dishing out. I would need the Armor of the believer spoken of which would prepare me for every battle and allow me to hold my ground. Ephesians 6:11 AMP Tells of it: Put on the God's whole armor [the armor of a heavy- armed soldier which God supplies], that you may be able successfully to stand up against [all] the strategies and the deceits of the devil. 12. For we are not wrestling with flesh and blood [contending only with physical opponents], but against the despotisms, against the powers against [the master spirits who are] the world rulers of this present darkness, against the spirit forces of wickedness in the heavenly (supernatural sphere.13. Therefore, put on God's complete armor, that you may be able to resist and stand your ground on the evil day [of danger], to stand [firmly in your place]. 14. Stand therefore [hold your ground], having tightened the belt of truth around your loins and having put on the breastplate of integrity and of moral rectitude and right standing with God. 15. And having shod your feet in preparation [to face the enemy with the firm footed stability the promptness and the readiness produced by the good news] of the gospel of peace. 16. Lift up over all the [covering shield of saving faith, upon which you can quench all the flaming missiles of the wicked [one]. 17. And take the helmet of salvation and the sword that the Spirit wields which is the Word of God. 18. Pray at all times and on every occasion, in every season) in the Spirit, with all manner of prayer and entreaty. To that end keep alert and watch with strong purpose and perseverance, interceding in behalf of all the saints. (God's consecrated people). This is the path to V-I-C-T-O-R-Y! Victory, Victory is our CRY! Shout it with me, I know you remember and if you don't join in NOW.

The Message version of the New Testament puts it in modern words. "A Fight to the Finish…. And that about wraps it up. God is strong and He wants you strong. So, take everything the master has set out for you, well made weapons of the best materials. And put them to use so that you will be able to stand up to everything the devil throws your way. This is no afternoon athletic contest that we'll walk away from and forget about in a couple of hours. This is for keeps, a life or death fight to the finish against the devil and all his demons.

Be prepared you are up against far more than you can handle on you own. Take all the help you can get, every weapon God has issued, so that when it is all over but the shouting, you'll still be on your feet. Truth, righteousness, peace, faith and salvation are more than words. Learn how to apply them. You'll need them throughout your life. God's word is an indispensable weapon. In the same way, prayer is essential for ongoing warfare. Pray hard and long. Pray for your brothers and sisters. Keep your eyes open. Keep each other's spirits up so that no on falls behind or drops out."

A cheerleader always, that's me. I just switched teams. Now I encourage God's team to faith and victory. I can see God's design and with his help you can too! Let Him take your good qualities refine them, and get you armed for the battle for your life and the lives of those you love and even your perceived enemies. Applying Truth, Righteousness, peace, faith, and salvation are the training of the Lord to give us the rewards and spoils of the victory already won by Christ. How great is it that we know the end of the story but can participate in the ending events of the history prophesied and written in scripture; motivated by His love to fight the good fight and sharing the spoils with Him as our inheritance from the Father?

Personally, my battle would intensify the more I proclaimed Gods testimonies of faithfulness. Seeking every opportunity for Divine appointments in everyday life, God would open doors to share hope, material goods, counsel, hospitality, counsel, prayers, encouragement. Frankly, more treasures than I can recount. Writing has opened my eyes to the pages of almost 40 years of recorded heights and depths recorded in my journals.

The journey likens to the story of "Much Afraid", a character in the dearly loved allegory, "Hinds Feet on High Places" by Hannah Hurnard. I have read it no less than four times along the way. Each reread has given insight to where I was currently journeying. I cannot say how many have received copies as gifts and received encouragement to read its pages of wisdom and realistic comparisons to walking with The Great Shepard, but I can say without doubt it is a life changing book.

Much Afraid is the main character. Lame and crippled, living in the Valley of Humiliation. A member of the Fearing family, who wants to escape their grip. She decides upon receiving the Great Shepard's invitation to follow him to the High Places, out of the reach of her relatives. Almost missing a meeting to proceed, because of distraction and bondage by relatives, her opportunity for Freedom, she breaks free with her voice, yelling for help in the form of her neighbor, Mrs. Valiant who comes to her aid. Much Afraid rushes to the trysting place to discuss plans. The Shepard is joyful that he is finally hearing her decision to go. "It would indeed be best for you." He states. "I will very willingly take you there myself. The lower slopes of those mountains on the other side of the river are the borderland of my Father's Kingdom, the Realm of Love. No Fears of any kind are able to live there because perfect love casteth out fear and everything that torments!"

She was concerned. Seeing the seed of Love in His Hand she spoke. "The seed looks very sharp," she said shrinkingly. "Won't it hurt if you put it into my heart?" He answered gently, "It is so sharp that it slips in very quickly. But much Afraid I have already warned you that Love, and Pain go together, for a time at least, If you would know Love you must know pain too."

Tears of sobbing intermixed with my words "No God not more pain! I don't want anymore pain. Life has been very painful." I had overlooked the "for a time at least" and recognizing them, hope and faith arose in my heart to continue following Him, granting permission of my will that He could do whatever it would take to bring me to the Kingdom. Everyone's life holds pain. Loss is at the root of it, because death of anything or anyone is loss. Suppression of feelings can result in many ills, addictions, broken relationships, suicides, acting out, treating others the way we have been treated, ignoring underlying effects and continuing cycles of past generations. In addition, there are things that we cannot explain but want answers.

Predominate among my struggles with fear of rejection, dislike for myself was right up there with it. Luke 10:27, Proverbs 23:7 and John 13 would all help in the healing the skewed perspective of my past. Familiarity with these passages needed to go beyond a mere "I have heard that before.", to the place of heartfelt knowledge and experience. God wants His word to become part of us. Hidden in our heart, so at any given moment we have His counsel for Life right there with us. Guiding us and using us to help guide others to Him. Self-Image needs to come from God's truth, not what is true from a world perspective. Every believer can enjoy the same riches of God's forgiveness (I Colossians 1:14, 2:13), of all our sins, having been paid in full and forgotten (Hebrews 10: 16-18) Eternal Life (John 17:3, I John 5: 11-13) and the indwelling of the Holy Spirit fulfill every promise of God through Christ Jesus. Along with our unique design, each of us have a special calling (Psalm 139, Ephesians 1, Psalm 40, Romans 12, and I Corinthians 12 will all agree to this statement. Ephesians 1, 4, 11, Isaiah 55 and Romans 8:28 agree on the Sovereignty (supreme rule and authority) of God. Finally, in Philippians 1:6 we are assured if we believe that God who has begun a good work in us will complete it.

Our cooperation and responsibility lie in Colossians 3, clearly, we are told to put to death and deprive the evil longings of our earthly body. All have sinned and fallen short of the Glory of God, (Romans 3:23) but Jesus provides the bridge to cross back over to relationship with Him. I John explains and if we step by step humbly confess and ask for help in our weakness, forgiveness is available until we see clear and the old self is put to death. True repentance changes our thoughts and ways to please Heavenly Father.

Intentionally passages references are meant to stir desire to know more for yourself: to confirm what I am writing as His witness. Christ is in control if we want him to be, and trust that He is: all that is needed to find Life worth living.

I was waiting for answers. Of course, we all have self-inflicted pain, and pain inflicted by others. And some of it is due to the truth that says the sins of the Father pass on to those who hate Him. Deuteronomy 5:9 is its origin. The TLB says it this way. You shall not bow down to any images nor worship them in anyway, for I am the Lord your God. I am a jealous God, and I will bring the curse of a father's sins upon even the third and fourth generation of the children of those who hate me; but I will show kindness to a thousand generations of those who love me and keep my commandments.

I wanted the "Buck to stop here" breaking the cycles generated by the generations of my heritage. Asking God to reveal those sins that had been passed to me through generational sins of my parents, grandparents, great grandparents, etc. I may have not been acquainted with my deceased relatives, but God was and could help me see how to gain forgiveness for their iniquity by taking responsibility to confess these sins. Passing the Buck is an expression popularized by U.S. President Harry Truman and Wikipedia says it comes from poker gameplay that came to mean "passing blame" or absolving oneself of responsibility or concern by denying authority or jurisdiction over a given matter. Jesus in his first appearance since his resurrection was recorded by the Apostle John in Chapter 20 verse 23 AMP [Now having received the Holy Spirit and being led and directed by Him] if you forgive the sins of anyone, they are forgiven; if you retain the sins of anyone they are retained.

Doing this cleans the archives and frees us and them, covering the sins with the blood of Jesus which the Father accepts as the sacrifice needed to absolve their future effects. It is important to do this for both mother and father and if you are married both spouses: cutting the chains of past generations in order that the devil no longer has legal ground spiritually to accuse you before Father God of being guilty unless of course you still act in that sinful attitude expressing it in your behavior which gives the devil legal right (we are acting "like the devil"). This action prevents continuance to your children. It is at this time you will remind the devil that the blood of Jesus covered all sins of the world if confessed and repented. My response was "Hit the road toad, I am forgiven!"

The decade of the eighties was a war filled decade for me, a prophetic word likened me to Joan of Arc. Whom I researched as leading her nation of France to victory in a hundred-year war. She was eighteen and believed God had called her through visions. Winning the approval of her people, who would eventually turn against her, she was victorious in battle, though paying the ultimate price of death by burning at the stake. She persevered to serve the God who called her.

The warrior likeness and call to war came to me generationally. My call however was spiritual not natural (physical). My maiden name of Hartman, of German descent, confirmed my warrior heritage background. Researching, after finding a Hartman coat of arms, purchased by my mother, I decided to honor my father on his 90th birthday with a presentation of a custom family crest, which I designed and assembled, based in the coat of arms and further research. Honored and elated, my father displayed it proudly and the crest has been shared with Hartman generations at our annual gathering. The coat of arms described the symbolism, one of which meant to God's glory.

One of the first battles, for His glory, took place the autumn after my new birth. It was quite a shock when my parents announced they were separating after 33 years of marriage. We all have shocks that send us into emotional waves of upset, trying to overtake us, I was no different, but I now realized I could go to God for help. The devil was behind this and I took responsibility to seek direction and possible involvement for reconciliation of their relationship. Conversations, with both Father and Mother, reminded them of the vows taken before God on their wedding day and responsibility to hold fast to their promises to one another. Changing their actions that lead to the separation, not allowing emotions control, but their promise to love through the worst of times. God showed me the process of reconciliation and within about a month they were back together and celebrated sixty-three years of marriage until Mom went home to heaven.

That was 1981. A lot of growth happened until the end of 1984 when our third child was twelve days past my due date. Feeling more than ready to deliver, the Christmas season was in full swing with planning family gatherings, shopping, wrapping and church events. I had already sought the Doctor to see if inducement was an option and asked the Lord to make it clear if this was to be my choice. Clearly, the Dr. emphatically told me that the birth process should be natural and unhurried. His demeanor, seen as God's indicator, let me know I would be waiting. Our baby would miss playing the baby Jesus in the pageant, but God's alternative child, as much a gift to the church, was a surprise the same as Mary's. It was perfect.

Aaron was our third son. From the beginning a sensitive and quieter personality than his older brothers. He decided to make his appearance on the 23rd at 4:15 am after we had been out celebrating a birthday with friends, until 1:00 am. Coming home, after a night of laughter and games, which I didn't want to end, I went to get ready for bed. Gary was taking care of the woodstove and while doing so, it became obvious, the time for baby's arrival was not long off. Contractions still not intense, we settled into bed. Gary exhausted, just got comfortable and was nodding off, suddenly I heard a popping noise and a contraction of very strong intensity was cause for the death grip of Gary's hand in mine. Contractions were coming every few minutes, providing comical scenes, while trying to get a coat and shoes on and get into the car. A second call to the Dr. who was not very pleasant, after 4 nights on delivery duty, told us to head to the hospital. He would meet us there. The name for a boy got an addition on the way, because if a boy he would be born on our friend's birthday. Of course, I was telling Gary to turn on the four -way blinkers and hurry it up! About halfway, on the 25- minute drive to Harrisburg Hospital, we passed the Doctor! Aaron Kyle Daniel Barr didn't take long to make his entrance into the world. We were over the moon with joy at his coming into our family. Wrapping him snuggly we tucked him into a huge Christmas stocking made by volunteers at the hospital, for pictures. Aaron uses that stocking every Christmas celebration. A 24 hour stay in the hospital and we returned home to happy siblings waiting to celebrate Christ's birth together. God is sooo Good!

At eight months of age Aaron would require surgery for crossed eyes and again prayer for God's involvement gave great results. After a first opinion, we decided on a second at the referred Will's Eye Hospital with a pediatric specialist. His diagnosis was unlike the other and I noticed differences, questioning them and seeking to understand. It was hard at first to even accept the need for surgery, we all view our children as perfect. However, submitting to the doctor's training, it was scheduled. My father was there with me and a great support. I was verbally declaring God's involvement and trusting Him to bring a desired healing for our son. Covering every doctor and nurse's involvement and the room with prayer by inviting the Lord to be part of everything. I was so happy to see a visible evidence when arriving home to familiar space, Aaron did a "double-take" when he saw the living room through both eyes for the first time. I was thankful for God's care, joyful for positive results.

Gary was working a part-time job with UPS and full-time with my Father's company to provide insurance. We lived most of our married years without insurance paying cash for any visits to doctors or ER, helping in effect to build our faith in God's provision for all we need. Being married with 3 dependents was new territory and unlike the provision I had experienced growing up. I was very co-dependent on my parents support financially, which would have to be addressed if I were to follow Christ and really learn to trust. My staying home to care for our children would return to test my willingness quite a few times when finances were tight or lacking and my anxiety turned to wanting to get a job. Always I would hear God say, "No, you will learn to trust me". I knew He wanted me to speak with my parents about not giving me so many material things. It was one of the hardest conversations I had with them and I am not sure at that time they understood but I know it was the beginning of trusting more deeply in my God who promises that His children will not lack any good thing. I was and continue to be amazed at the provisions of my Father. I give thanks for my natural father whom God chose for the job, as the imparter of my ability to believe for great provision because this was the example I saw as a child.

1985, was a year of many challenges in our faith. I would go to the hospital, one night, thinking I was having a heart attack. Pain down my left arm, shortness of breath, these led us to the ER around midnight. Mom accepted the call for child care in the wee hours of morning. Hours of testing showed nothing more than anxiety: a reality that made me know my faith needed to take me deeper into the love of Christ. I was trying to home school and take care of two very young children and be the exemplary wife, and housekeeper at the same time! We all know of the "Super-Mom" image that our culture has embodied. I too, overloaded myself with expectations way above the level of peaceful feelings and circumstance. Always hard on myself, I sabotaged peace and rest by holding myself to expectations that overloaded my schedule and wore down my health. God knew I needed structure and as I prayed to have it, opportunity through church came to do a seminar on "Becoming an Organized Woman". What a novel idea! Coming away with tools to give me structure bringing more peace to my soul and home, I was studious and determined to achieve the goal. There were some extreme measures I did not implement such as giving my husband a minute by minute schedule of my entire day! It is not that difficult to understand that extremes as such are a burden, as Christ said his burden was, light and easy. Focus and coming back, again and again to the schedule I created, were necessary until it became habit. Eventually, I was able to flow and adjust as needed but remaining true to tasks appropriated for specific days. Mondays and Thursdays, laundry, and Cleaning Friday. Shopping Saturday etc. I had to force the habit until I had the desire and saw the results of being organized. My mantra became "A place for everything and everything in its place!"

That way I would know where something was and didn't have to
search. Just recently I was encouraged by a Facebook post to watch
Tidying Up with Maria Kondo. I was inspired to take some of my
organization further. I saw and felt good that a lot of what she did
I had already implemented, but reality is that life brings changes
that require reorganization and decluttering. Recently, my last
child moved out and now I could use my entire home. It is a work
in progress and yet, not difficult if skills and habit are established.
Whatever we are privy too in learning, not all of it will fit us, but
that is why we enter the "field" and glean and take away what is
profitable to the edification of our being.

Gary was employed still with my father's company when my
youngest brother was brought on as Sales Manager and promoted
in Summer 1985 to President while my father remained CEO.
Having worked closely with my dad, he shared his insecurity
of a lack of higher education in business, but he had grown
a successful company to that point which was on the path of
transition from medium to large production capabilities and
decided that my brother was his choice to make the transition, he
did have an MBA, showed qualities of leadership and potential
for the company's expected growth in the future. My two older
brothers were in management as well: production and marketing.
With difficulty, I realized that the dream of becoming a woman
executive, president in the family business, would pass and feelings
of jealousy and competition would have to be overcome with
understanding and forgiveness. It was a good thing the news came
while on vacation in my happy place, the beach. Surely, God was
aware that it would help me to enter into his presence to find his
desire to bless my brother, and remind me, I was so blessed to be a

stay at home mother of three beautiful sons, a desire which I had many years before the women's lib movement put the thought of company president in the picture.

Meanwhile continuing fellowship with the same church group, a decision to seek a different type of governing structure required a vote between a board or biblical Apostles and prophets who gave guidance. The final vote would split the church body causing many to begin a new fellowship under an organization following an Apostolic and prophetic model. They were one of the first to replicate and as such still had to figure out how and what that modern-day prototype included. Our family decided that we wanted to explore the possibilities with others of like mind and that our pastor's heart was under the leadership of the Holy Spirit. The transition was subtle and about a year long process before questions of confusion arose in the minds and hearts of some as our pastor was asked to step down from leadership for reasons none of us could grasp. Prior to this we all saw and felt the love and fruit of the Holy Spirit in the ministry, however, the pastor encouraged us to submit to the process and hoped that we would soon be at peace.

A short time passed, and the roles of male/female, came forth as control of man not the Holy Spirit and felt to me a lot like a prison not freedom to be my creative, less structured personality. Prayer and fasting were necessity to see my way through the confusion to God's intention for my life. The time spent would reveal to my heart the call of the Lord on my life prophetically as intercessor. Highlighted in my search were Ezekiel 3, which would strengthen my resolve to obey, knowing my words would be held to account. Also, Jeremiah 6 showing my purpose to rebuild the broken places of the soul to glorify Jesus and help the body to come to wholeness through intervention and relationship. So, warrior and bridge builder became my call. Hartman and Barr, warrior and bridge, prophetically foretold my purpose far before I was aware of the implications of my name. It also revealed that a discussion with leadership was necessary and that we would uphold to them the truth of the extremes we felt were not biblical, requiring us to remove ourselves from membership.

During these couple years, I experienced training by the Holy Spirit in warfare and saw him move prophetically by a word of knowledge that came forth through me during worship. There was someone in the congregation who was thinking about suicide. It would be after the service had ended; a young girl approached me for prayer saying the word was about her. Beginnings of discipling and relationship took root. She would be my first disciple for Christ. Teaching and training, we spent time on the phone and in my home. She was flourishing and began to express her joy in the friendship to her mother. Abruptly jealousy subdued our contact even though I had freely expressed pure intentions for our relationship. No matter, God would work in her life despite my own lack of involvement and I would pray. A couple of years later at age 15 after a time apart we saw each other, in a restaurant, and she expressed the dire circumstance of emotional abuse she felt and was thinking of leaving home. I only expressed that if she needed me, I would be there for her. It wasn't long before she came to our home for refuge, pushing me into more prayer and fasting for answers to the situation. A conversation Friday with her mother made me think she was supportive of our desire to bring reconciliation, but Saturday's call was altogether another spirit.

A meeting of parties to discuss her welfare placed my soul of fear into the hands of God to trust that the words he gave me to speak would have His desired effect. Again, I released this vulnerable girl to God's care, and He put her in another home of refuge, agreed upon by daughter and parents. He had protected her and put her in a place of safety and increased learning, to trust and discern His will for her life. Our love for one another is still alive.

Remaining tied to the fellowship for the next 3 years saw hard lessons of learning to discern appropriate leader authority and role recognition as a person, wife and mother. It was leadership that seemed good at first but later began to wreak havoc with pressures to conform and disallow individuality. A pressure cooker of control which felt like a force pushing me into a box into which I was not made to fit. I watched my previous friend who was very gifted and successful, be demoted in ministry and leave in emotional torment. Women who were more outgoing like me were told it wasn't acceptable. And ministry was relegated to those who would get in the box. I prayed asking the Lord to make clear to us where it was, we were to be; to guide us through the confusion and hurt of all. Gene Edwards wisely puts into words the question many ask in such situations. "The man I sit under: I think he is a King Saul. How can I know with certainty?"

Our Nation faces such even now. To answer he continues:

"It is not given us to know. And remember, even Sauls are often the Lord's anointed.

You see, there are always men-everywhere, in every age, and in every group- who will stand and tell you: "That man is after the order of King Saul." While another, just as sure, will rise to declare "No he is the Lord's anointed after the order of David." No man can *really* know which of the two is correct. And if you happen to be in the balcony looking down at those two men screaming at one another, you many wonders to which order, if any, *they* belong.

Remember, your leader may be a David.

"That's impossible!"

Is it? Most of us know at least two men in the lineage of David Who have been damned and crucified by men. Men who were absolutely certain the men they were crucifying were *not* Davids.

And if you don't know of two such cases for sure you know of one.

Men who go after the Sauls among us often crucify the Davids among us.

Who, then, can know who is a David and who is a Saul?

God knows. But He won't tell.

Will you be so certain your king is a Saul and not a David that you are willing to take the position of God and do war against your Saul? If so then let us thank God, you did not live in the days when Golgotha was in use.

What then can you do? Very little. Perhaps nothing.

However, the passing of time and the behavior of your leader while that time passes) reveals a great deal about your leader.

And the passing of time, and the way you react to that leader-be he David or Saul-reveals a great deal about you.! Let God handle them because he will if they are not of his camp.

We will as humanity untransformed by the power of God be tempted to take control, but God if we let him will bring sweet vindication when we step aside from judgment and pray for the will of the Father to be accomplished. Wait as Isaiah 26:8 says, "Yes on the path of your judgement O Lord, we wait [expectantly] for

You; our heartfelt desire is for Your name and the remembrance of You."

A strategy like this was what I required for my next spiritual battle, requiring again fasting and prayer and obedience to intervene in very discomforting events happening within the family and family business. Shortly after his installment as president, my brother sought to acquire the help of a business consultant, Dr. Miller out of Chicago. It was the current business trend taking root in the affairs of corporate America and securing such came with a hefty price tag, one which was even greater than the bill attached to his consulting. A total restructure from the top executives down to the labor force even including executive wives. It was the winter of 1986, when the process began. My mother was not in agreement and rejected his philosophy, Freudian psychology in nature. Her resistance did not affect the determination of my father and brothers to continue his involvement, including tools of subliminal suggestion via recordings listened to while asleep. Gaining agreement of my father who gave him authority to do whatever he thought necessary to make the company powerful and successful was a fatal move. A move I would later discern as the open door the enemy used along with greed to ruin an otherwise prosperous manufacturing company.

Infiltrating the ranks of employees, from top to bottom, the wickedness of destructive forces in the spirit realm were utilizing whatever means to steal, rob, kill and destroy my natural inheritance. Months would pass before awareness came through Gary who was now subjected to the indoctrination already crumbling company foundations and pillars, causing a chain reaction of firing, lawsuits, confusion, broken promises and chaos that extended to personal family.

Gary and fellow workers were called to meetings that lasted hours, where Dr. Miller and his right-hand man, Serge, tried to push their philosophy. Lewd jokes, and insinuating comments about women's body parts were common faire. Gary decided upon the word perverted to describe Dr. Miller and his actions. When questioned by the woman, who somehow got the promotion which my dad had promised Gary, asked him "What do you think of Dr. Miller?" His answer? "Perverted!" Unsuspecting of a plot to use his very words, to slay him, until a phone call for an Amway order, requested a stop by the main offices. Arriving to seek out the order, a brother told him to have a seat in the near-by office while he got it.

Within minutes, Dr. Miller, Serge, and two of my brothers filed in. The desk drawer was opened, and the click of a recorder was heard. Then Dr. Miller proceeded forward to proximity of Gary's face. Gary was still seated. In forceful angry words, Dr. Miller spoke. "If you ever slander my name again, I will take care of you. We have people who will take care of you. And your family! You better watch what curb you step off!" Gary recalls a force holding him in his seat, keeping him from what his natural man wanted him to do in reaction which was punch his lights out.

This all happened in January of 1986, but Gary didn't reveal it until 3 weeks had passed and the effects of the confrontation had caused me to notice a marked change in Gary's demeanor. Nervous and pacing a lot, quieter than usual, I questioned. "What is wrong, you have been acting unusually strange?" He was broken from carrying the weight of woundedness and disappointment and worry. Sharing the event in the above detail, I was literally in shock and disbelief that my family would betray family to this degree.

Immediately my response was to say that "My father couldn't possibly have known and agreed with this type of action! You need to call him at home and ask to go in for a talk." Gary agreed and made the call, which was received, and invitation extended to come. At home I waited with bated breath, not thinking I would hear the words of my father's reply after Gary's outpouring of the event. "Of course, I knew! It was a ploy to get you to come over to our side."

My mind and emotions were swirling in the implications of this betrayal and not long into it I knew it was time to arm myself for battle by praying and seeking God's answer to stop this upheaval of destruction. I didn't know this man, my father, who would go to extreme wicked lengths. God spoke. "Susan you need to remove your father from the throne of your heart. I am the only one who should be on the throne!" I replied in tears, "Yes, my Lord, forgive me, only you are Worthy." Progress toward Kingdom.

Weeks of heartfelt seeking for the answer finally produced a rhema word. Lead to read Deuteronomy 11: 22-25, the verses revealed God's plan. I knew what He was asking me to do, but this seemed huge and my response was "God? This sounds a lot like Joshua and Jericho." I would continue praying, asking for confirmation, which God says is the way to know that you know.

Sunday following would bring the first. A new song! The words taken directly from the very same verses God had given me… the second, only days later quoted on a Christian radio station. No argument from me. I was convinced. Now when and how became the focus of eventual obedience. When God calls us, He will make the way plain. Clearly, he had done so for me.

That Spring Gary and I had taken responsibility to mow every one of my father's properties. The promise to deliver to me the land where I set the soles of my feet made perfect sense. Armed with those verses as my command and Matthew 18:18 KJV Verily, I say unto you, Whatsoever ye shall bind on earth shall be bound in heaven: and Whatsoever ye shall loose on earth shall be loosed in heaven. And, the Covenant of the Blood of Christ that gave me authority over every demon, NIV I have given you authority to trample on snake and scorpions and to overcome all the power of the enemy; nothing will harm you. I marched and declared with faith, Binding Satan and all his cohorts from any further action of destruction and releasing the Holy Spirit to accomplish it all! Trusting God would deliver it to me. That was the end of April 1986.

The next six weeks, all hell broke loose, family marriages were breaking, and one saved from another affair, accountants were declaring the need to sell or go bankrupt, and Gary was handed a handwritten letter of resignation and "forced" to sign it. Me? I was at peace in my soul. God was doing what I ask in saving my family from further destruction and influence from Dr. Miller. I knew Gary would find another job, because God is good. I also had no idea of the outcome.

July arrived and I was walking in forgiveness and grace. I knew who the enemy was and it wasn't my family. A visit to my parent's home disclosed Dr. Miller's exit. My father said he had news. Oh! "Yes, Dr. Miller died today, of a massive heart attack."

My mind trying to grasp what was said and yet my spirit heard shouting and rejoicing. What was the conflicting reaction?

I never imagined that outcome, but certainly his philosophy and influence was now destroyed. Hallelujah! I asked the Lord to speak to me on the way home, to show me why my mind thought "Too bad." And my spirit heard shouts and rejoicing. Opening my Bible my eyes fell on the page and read this verse. Proverbs 11:10 NIV When the righteous prosper, the city rejoices; when the wicked perish there are shouts of joy! That settled it for me. But that would not be the end of the consequences to our family.

CHAPTER 5 🌿

Pruning and Cutting

Have you ever considered the unfurling of a rosebud, as each petal gives itself in absolute surrender to the process of being uncovered?

—Catherine Brown

I am my Love's and he is mine,
And this is his desire
That with his beauty I many shine
In radiant attire.
And this will be—when all of me
Is pruned and purged with fire.

—Cant. 7:10-13 (Hinds Feet on High
Places/Hannah Hurnard

Being aware of God's unfolding, sensitivity to his voice, and touches, His creation comes into my soul in ways I could have never previously imagined prior to our relationship. Difficulties of sight, in mind and vision, were painful to examine but His pruning had to move me toward His perspective. Pruning a rose removes diseased and dead unproductive parts to encourage growth. My life needed a severe pruning to remove bouts with selfishness, laziness inconsistency, self-pity, depression, unrighteous anger, rejection syndrome. All of these had to leave, and time would tell if my surrender to His work would yield the beauty He desired.

The whole of my life thus far would serve as the ground for hard cuts, but my faith romance with Jesus never seemed to dull and the pain be so great as to make me quit the process of growth. Each trial and test served to deepen my resolve to experience life as He intended. The hardest was yet to come.

My brother, closest in age, moved across the United States to Southern California, May of 1988. But before he would leave, I would give him a new niece. Late August of 1986, carrying her became news. Hoping for a daughter but knowing it was God's will that I wanted, we chose the names Laura Kate and Alexander Wayne. Loving "Little House on the Prairie", the character Laura reminded me of myself; a tomboy inquisitive and high spirited with a penchant for storytelling. Kate was the name of a beautiful girl from childhood church. Alexander Wayne combined the middle names of our fathers. No matter, God would honor my desires.

The day was September 30, my mother's 53rd birthday and I wanted to get her a copy of my favorite book, "Hinds Feet on High Places". Off to the mall, childcare in place, I was feeling lighthearted and free. I knew just where to find it in the bookstore and didn't take too long to purchase and continue, on my light-hearted way through the mall. Considering thoughtfully the growing child within, I started a conversation with the Lord. "You know if you give me a baby girl, I am going to name her Laura Kate." Stopped dead in my tracks and looking skyward as His response came clear and with audible voice. "If I give you a baby girl, I don't want you to name her Laura Kate."

"Well what do you want me to name her?" The conversation seemed as normal as any in the moment. He spoke again. "Hannah". As I quickly considered his name, I responded, "Oh that's a pretty name." but what about Gary?" meaning we never seemed to agree on names. Pondering I answered my own question, speaking it back to Him. "Ok, If I know you God then I know I won't have to convince Gary, you will already have spoken to him just like you told Joseph about Jesus name and Zachariah about John's." It was very clear and no more was said. Emotionally high and my faith enlarged, my new experience with Jesus, would birth a testimony of His goodness that I spoke of most everyday following until her arrival.

Nestled in bed and having our nightly conversation, I broke the news to Gary, his first question was "How do you know that?"

"God spoke to me today", I replied

Repeating word for word what was spoken during my encounter, Gary responded with the exact words I had said. There was no doubt, *we were having a baby girl and her name would be Hannah*. She would be a testimony of God's love and grace to me, embraced and covered with a name given by Him that means "Divine Grace".

God does not disappoint. Hebrews 10: 23 the Open Bible says this, "Let us hold fast to the confession of our hope without wavering, for he who promised is faithful." I would believe his words. He would not have spoken at all if he did not intend to fulfill them: God does not dangle carrots. A baby girl was coming to join our already beautiful family of three very loved boys.

Traveling my path in the coming months would give never ending opportunity to share my story. Musing from those noticing my belly would include "I guess you are hoping for a girl this time." Opening the door for my conversation with God about her name. This always made me smile as reactions were comical. "Oh, you did, did you?" and sarcastically, "Oh, that's interesting." There were those who shared faith and were interested to hear and encourage me saying "that is quite a testimony!". I knew the treasure I held in my heart. He has treasures for all his children.

Our due date was April 16th and three weeks before a small get away to Baltimore Inner Harbor and my oldest cousin Mary Ann's home was just what we needed. Rest and relaxation. MaryAnn gave her life to Christ at a Billy Graham crusade and was a spiritual pillar for me. She offered spiritual insight and caring, offering Christ's open arms of love. Even when I showed up unexpectedly at her door one night in tears from marital discord. She set me back on the straight and narrow path with God's guidance and told me "You need to go home!" I appreciated her frank attitude based in God's word. Sunday plans included worship and her delicious home cooking. Waking up early, I noticed I felt somewhat unusual. An R.N., MaryAnn asked "You aren't going into labor, are you?"

"I don't think so. I am not due for three weeks." Replying with the knowledge that all my other deliveries were past the due date. Church and dinner were refreshing, and the afternoon of conversation passed quickly. Time for us to begin the hour and a half journey to PA came too quickly, ending a much-needed time away from normal routine with joyful family fellowship... Our boys would be excited to see us and we them. Friends from church who also had two children volunteered to stay at our house. We were sure the activity of five boys would make our return welcome.

Barely enroute, contractions started coming at regular intervals. Could it be labor? Time would tell. Continuing even as we arrived home, our excitement elevated as the possibility of Hannah's birth could occur on Gary's mother's birthday. Another amazing circumstance. God had spoken to me on my mother's birthday and to think she could be born on my mother-in-law's was something only God could arrange.

The boys were excited to see us, the prospect of the arrival of their sister heightened their energies. Steve and Vicki were more than happy to rearrange schedules to accommodate additional care for the boys after we were certain a trip to the hospital was forthcoming. At 10pm, circumstance dictated time to go to the hospital. Our waiting hearts and arms were ready to receive this most precious gift. Midnight came and assured us that her Grammy would have a real BIG surprise for her birthday. One she would not forget.

Labor was slow. Dr. Woodward shared that often between 3rd and 4th deliveries abdominal weakness increased length of labor. No sleep for us. My desire to deliver was overtaken by exhaustion and at 7 am, tears! The freshened staff was perky and had brought some much-needed encouragement, but I thought prayers would help speed the labor and calm my emotions. Calling the prayer warriors, via Vicki, my mother, whose ears heard my sobs, announced my desire for the end of labor and the birth to be over. Mom was encouraging and after a short conversation I was calmed.

Within twenty minutes of putting out the call to prayer, God was answering. Labor intensified and within 40 minutes I was ready to birth. After the final push, I looked to see her, but I thought it was a boy and voiced it. Quickly in unison, the Doctor, Nurses and Gary spoke, "Oh no it isn't, it is a beautiful baby girl!" and my heart filled with Joy... Hannah Christine was born: my testimony confirmed. Faith is the substance of things hoped for and evidence of things not seen. KJV Hebrews 11:1 "Divine grace and anointed one" Our first call would be to Grammy only 4 minutes after birth. "Happy Birthday, Mom! You have a new Granddaughter!" Both of us were crying tears of joy. Hannah and her Grammy would celebrate their birthdays for many years in bonded love for one another through the time until 2015 when Hannah relocated to Alaska to teach and location prohibited physical togetherness. Hannah was indeed special; she was the first girl granddaughter after 80 successive grandsons born in the Barr family. Life did hold goodness and my heart was grateful. My reality was not the painful past but evolving into satisfaction with positive decisions to turn away from sin and structures of my past, examining effects, then venturing toward my true self. The struggle sometimes was overwhelming. But then God's rewards would come as a healing balm to show me progressive goodness.

Generosity abounded from family and church, with meals for two weeks and a shower that blessed us with "all things girl!". Meanwhile Gary was transitioning into the construction trades and decided to learn computer technology through evening school, leaving me as the sole caregiver of our four little ones. Quite a challenge to my skills at management but offering opportunity to grow strong in character.

Perfectionism had to go as it drove me to keep pace in wanting an immaculate house, excellent meals on a tight budget, clothes of high quality (mostly the children's purchased by mom and dad), and trying to be a good wife, mother and friend. All the while keeping a vibrant relationship with the Lord.

Coming to terms with that required introspection and determination. Creativity I didn't realize before Christ started to come forth. When the house got too messy for emotional comfort, we created a game...300 second pick-up. For those seconds we would as a family attack the mountain of disarray helping to relieve the stress of chaos. I had read a verse that stated where chaos dwells there is every sort of evil. Not something I wanted for sure!

Education of our children was something else we had to determine. Many at church were opting for homeschool and it was a consideration for us. Researching the options, I read recommended books and decided with the support I could probably do the elementary grades. Ten years post grad education accounted for some confidence to teach elementary principles. Studies showed boys to be better in a structured setting at an older starting age. We decided on enrollment, waiting at least until the age of six, for the younger four. Ben already had started in a pre-school at age 4. I took on his kindergarten curriculum and was overwhelmed with responsibilities apart from schooling.

Fourteen loads of laundry just one. Revising plans, he attended private Christian school for first and second grade. The cost was prohibitive and so 3rd grade I tried homeschooling again, with outside science, music and physical ed. Nathan and Aaron were toddlers of 3 and 2 years and Hannah was on her way. By mid-autumn the following year I literally broke down emotionally from overload of responsibility. My energy sapped and thinking burned. I wanted to quit life.

The acceptance of responsibility broke me. But then God showed up in a good friend, spent an evening listening to my plight, in a parked car, in the dark of night, as her wisdom gave me hope from fear of failure. Failure was not part of who I wanted to be. But it became evident to me, God did not require me to fit expectations real or assumed that made me feel a prisoner. She was a homeschooler and yet by her very gracious attitude she set me free, deciding then it was okay to enroll Ben in the public school where I had attended. My somewhat immature unstructured creative nature needed to develop into more structure for my sanity. The timing of our conversation was exactly what I longed to hear and the next day Ben was enrolled. Whew, more freedom to be who I truly was. Two toddlers and an infant were enough without school too.

There were days when anticipation of Gary's arrival home was putting me on the edge. Hopefully I would soon calm down and realize...this too shall pass. Worry had not been part of my growing up years because my parents spoiled me and took care of all my needs allowing me to be carefree. Adulthood was full of cares and responsibility. None of which I was emotionally prepared to handle.

I would learn how to thrift shop for clothing and groceries. My sister-in-law opened my eyes on a trip to a Pittsburgh Goodwill. I was amazed at the brand quality and newness of items that could be purchased at a fraction of their retail cost. We did have a Christian food bank where if help was necessary and it was a few times, we could receive groceries. It was there that we learned about a discount grocery not far and very inexpensive. BB's Bent and Dent was located on an Amish farm in an outbuilding with two aisles and an attached gas fired freezer. Most everything was in date, prices were so reasonable and allowed us to enjoy some special treats like the Entennmen's cheese cakes, a Philadelphia bakery, in the freezer that sold for .50. Cheesecake was a favorite of mine from childhood as Sunday dinner usually included semi-frozen (that's the way we liked it) Sarah Lee. We had plenty of room in a 1940's ice cream freezer that we purchased at auction for $3.00. Yep, $3.00. Never knowing if they would be available, the next shopping trip, I sometimes purchased $5.00 worth, earning me a new title, "Susie Cheesecake".

The freezer found by the purchase of the Davis' house by my younger brother, had originally sat in Davis' Drug Store, on main street of my hometown, loaded with delicious flavors of ice cream in five gallon containers behind the Soda fountain counter where soda jerks scooped and made the most delicious root beer floats to be had and the stools of red "pleather" swirled in circles taking you past the float for sips on your ride! This freezer had memories! The double flip doors would continue to open to goodness, only now it was cheesecake, pizza and homemade applesauce, good memories of childhood. Eventually the cheesecake became a treat enjoy more rarely. Treats were abundant so learning to appreciate them as such required not having them as often and one that was always around was pizza.

Our free pizza stopped with the end of the business so paying for them was a shock. Taking 28 years of free and saying good-bye was like going through withdrawal. A rude awakening at least.

But following Jesus is about leaving things behind to find the true fulfillment of the soul. Experiencing loss to find meaning. Finding meaning to enter the purposes for your life. I would survive and thrive…eventually. This pruning stuff was painful for the moment.

September 1987, we planned a celebration of my parent's 40th Anniversary. An event we were blessed to share considering the past and now to celebrate victory of the momentous occasion. Did I say I like party planning? My dream job in heaven would be "God's Party Planner. Gary came down on the day of the party with a violent headache, requesting I take him to the hospital. I prayed and sensed that God was saying he wasn't physically sick, but it was related to a sin issue. Telling him what I had heard God say, he should take it into consideration while I attended the party. If after, he still wanted to go to the hospital, I would take him. Two hours passed, a phone call to my brother's was for me, "Hello", it was Gary. "We need to talk when you get home, God showed me the problem and I need to confess."

My imagination gone wild, the children had been tucked in and now we could talk. He began telling me that he fell into temptation. A high school friend asked if he could store some boxes in our barn at the farm. Gary agreed. At some point, most likely the move, the contents revealed pornographic magazines. Gary succumbed to temptation and this sin was what God was after. This felt like a bad movie, a betrayal of our marriage vows to keep ourselves only for each other. Trust was broken, my heart hurt deeply. Forgiveness needed to come, and trust rebuilt. Marriage counseling with Abundant Living was our lifeline. Norm and Betty Charles, former missionaries, wrote a book, "Heaven on Earth, Family Style". Opening a counseling center near us to help marriages heal and grow was their goal. Hopefully they could help us find trust again.

Anxiety was very real for me, beside the trip to the ER, when stress was revealed as the culprit. The combination of circumstances financially and martially added up too much and was an area I needed to grow. My life verse at the intersection was in Proverbs 3:5 Trust in the Lord with all your heart and lean not on your own understanding. In all your ways acknowledge Him and He will direct your path. NKJV

It seemed there was always a test to be passed but then I had to agree tests toward growth were the means to the end. Growth into maturity was my aim. Giving in faith to overcome worry about lack. The extremes were counter and the latter bondage. The just shall live by faith stated the place of hope and prosperity for the soul. Will I ever find God's freedom? Can I exercise my faith on a daily basis? These were questions only to be answered through discipline by my heavenly Father. Somedays opening the refrigerator stressed me and weeks when there was no money for groceries sent my levels of anxiety to heights I had not known. Matt 6:26 spoke loudly about trusting God for provision. Overcoming my desire to fix it for myself by going to work outside the home entered my thoughts often, especially during transitions. But God…He would help me make my home a river of giving and hospitality as his answer to my getting a job outside became a clear once again "Not now Susan, you will learn to trust me."

Resources that allowed me to do home parties, filled the void, I had the retail experience and a support system of friends willing to buy from me instead of retailers allowed for success and provision. Parties provided clothing, décor, kitchen necessities, all keeping me right where God wanted me… at home with my husband and children. At the same time Thrift stores provided for other needs.

During that trip to Pittsburgh in Spring '88, God would awaken me to understand other's perspectives on how I shared my faith. While my sister-in-law and I prepared dinner, our conversation included sharing my faith. She and my brother were now divorced, it was only the two of us and baby Hannah. I loved sharing God's work in me and telling of the victorious changes in my life, why I know he is the only way to Life. None of what I shared was wrong, only my delivery which seemed forced and intimidating from her perspective. Agitation appeared laying some heart felt words of her own on the table which caused me to feel rejected. No mind was paid to my own abrupt words that made her feel the same. Retreating, tears rolling down my cheeks, I sought safety in my bedroom. Consolation would come through prayer and repentance once I realized my mistake. Picking up a book I brought, Freedom of Simplicity by Richard J. Foster, I prayed asking for insight into what had just happened. Not long into my search, becoming quiet in my soul and thinking introspectively about my reading, Holy Spirit began to enlighten my mind.

"Silence frees us from the need to control others. One reason we can hardly bear to remain silent is that it makes us feel so helpless. We are accustomed to relying on words to manage and control others. A frantic stream of words flows from us in an attempt to straighten others out. We want so desperately for them to agree with us to see things our way. We evaluate people, judge people, condemn people. We devour people with our words. Silence is one of the deepest disciplines of the Spirit simply because it put a stopper on that. When we become quiet enough to let go of people, we learn compassion for them."

Going on to say that one of the levels of maturity as a believer we will go through is sharing our faith with sincerity of heart but in a rather insincere approach, with regard to the person to whom we are speaking. Boom! The gavel came down in that moment, judging me to be in the wrong approach. "Please forgive me Lord and help me to share what you have just shown me."

Breakfast came and I was given opportunity to humbly share. Asking her forgiveness for my approach and sharing with her the divine intervention of circumstance that had brought that book to be with me in Pittsburgh. Reconciliation was at hand. However, this is one of those times that afterward requires the silence of letting go. That's a hard lesson for one like myself. Anyone who knows me knows I love talking but the talking needed tempered and forged in the wisdom of God so others could hear without all the clanging of unnecessary wordiness, amidst the still buried wounds and emotions I still harbored.

Proverbs 10 is a wealth of wisdom for learning to control one's tongue. After all, God declares the tongue can be tamed by no man. Read James 3. Which tells us that wisdom from above is First of all pure (undefiled); then it is peace loving, courteous (considerate, gentle). It is willing to yield to reason, full of compassion and good fruits; it is wholehearted and straight forward, impartial and unfeigned (free from doubts, wavering and insincerity). Only by the undeserved grace of God would I learn this wisdom, in hope that God would bear its fruits in my life. Sorting out the details of the process may seem immense for us, but it is hardly anything difficult for Him.

Opening my being (mind, will and emotions) to the light of His word was the only path to transformation. Just like a flashlight that brightens the darkness to find something hidden and lost, God's word shines within us to reveal the lost and hidden person among the thorns and briars, to reveal his original design for each. My words and intonation would require many times of repentance until compassion replaced them. My mouth had earned me the nickname "Sister-sandpaper". I could accept that if my words were tempered by the Holy Spirit. Susan Bizarre was another nickname I received, but then God says we are a peculiar people. If it made people feel better to name-call I wasn't going to let it bother me when I knew they were only uncomfortable with God's truth in me.

May of 1988 my closest brother and Dad would travel together for his move to So. California. We had connections with family there so it would help him transition to a new place and business career. Brad was starting a lawn and landscape company, with roses as his new logo. He was in search of freedom and peace after the botched business decision. I loved that he had the courage to start over. I did not think I would have ever chosen to move 3000 miles from home. Brad's farewell party was filled with mixed emotion, happiness for his new adventure, sadness that he would no longer be within our close community. Getting used to that would be hard for me as we had only reconciled and become close within the prior few years. His dreaded Mother's Day departure saw Brad and Dad driving off in a U-Haul with all his belongings to find his dreams in the California Sunshine State.

But if not for that, our lives would not have been enriched to increase of effort to not lose touch, realizing now if we really loved him; we would have to make the time to show him with calls, letters, pictures and visits. He was good too, keeping in touch with letters and regular weekly phone calls. Our lives revealed desire to keep relationship alive.

Before Brad's move, earlier in April, Gary completed his two-year Computer Tech program and was job hunting. That journey would take two years before acquiring a position in 1990 with Sun Electric as a field tech in Bridgeton NJ. A position which would require a family change of address. Expecting our fifth child, a son, known only because God spoke to me during a sentimental moment of thoughts concerning the end of Hannah's baby days. I didn't want them to end. He spoke "It's okay to let go, you will have another son." I kept it tucked away in my heart waiting for the time to come. Now only months from his arrival, we would have to find a house and then relocate to a totally unknown area. This experience would certainly peel down any remaining co-dependencies, thereby strengthening interdependency on God and new community. Yearning to know the reality of His words that when I am weak, He is strong would hopefully gird me for the days ahead in a new land.

Driving a "For Sale by Owner" sign by road on our lot stirred emotion. Fear, excitement, surfacing insecurities, thrust me deeper into trust. Relying on others for affirmation, wisdom and emotional support seemed always afar off. But Christ had been close in the early years of my commitment. Teaching me to be watchful and discerning of the actions of myself and others. I had trusted wrongly in the past, way too much, no boundaries led to the mess I became and created. His boundaries were teaching safe relational skills, nourishing the ground of my roots.

A day trip to Bridgeton NJ with Gary, to check available housing netted a suitable prospect. I had already searched out likely worship centers and talked with a pastor. On a beautiful small lake, sat a craftsman style house, the details were the stuff of my dreams, and if moving had to be, this seemed a comfort in the midst of angst. Lake activities, like boating, swimming, fishing all seemed like possible enjoyment for our growing family. I was willing to move, yet my emotions were not aligned with reality.

Leaving home to travel was never a problem because I knew I would return to comfortable, familiar surroundings in my hometown. Daddy made sure we experienced culture outside of our Pennsylvania German heritage, taking us across country in 1966 hitting a lot of states and seeing new sights and eating new foods. As an adult, I was privileged to visit Belgium, Mexico, East and West Caribbean, including more of the U.S, Alaska, NH, Florida, and Texas. Pennsylvania offered changing seasons. Sparkling snow, sledding, ice skating, snow-forts and snowball fights were winters pleasures and Spring came forth with budding of chartreuse leaves, flowering dogwood, magnolia, and gardens of enormous perennial beauty. Temperatures were pleasant, bringing the end of the winter hibernation of animals, birds and some people, me specifically. Time to be outside and feel fresh air, and beauty stirring life within and without. Nestled in a Valley between two mountain ranges, Summer came with heat, rain, and humidity (which I still don't relish), but swimming, hiking, horseback riding, and summer delicacies of fresh fruit and vegetables covered any disappointment with the heat. Autumn painted the mountains and trees with shades of colored leaves, burgundy, rose, gold, in varying tones, winds following the fall rains brought abandonment of branches leaving them striped of their former glory. It was time for campfire dinners, smores and sweats.

The Valley is beautiful. Scattered with many dairy farms, silos breaking the skyline, and family homes, some from the inception of the town. Small business is a part of the economy and is growing. The college, LVC, provides culture, concerts, art gallery and sporting events. The updated campus adds amenities such as a sports center, college library and tennis courts. Annville experienced a renewal and is now a destination for date night with several restaurants, the Allen Theatre, remodeled completely from childhood, and coffee shop. Boasting the state's largest Memorial Day Parade when patriotism floods the streets for three hours of show, filled with respect for men and women who serve or have served our country. Bands, singing, lots of flags, enormous amounts of Army equipment, soldiers, horses, floats from local business, more, all viewed and appreciated by members of the surrounding communities. These were the stuff of years of good memories; leaving would be a major emotional and physical challenge.

Plans to secure the purchase of the house were set for November 3, 1990. However, God had other plans for us, as labor to deliver our 5th child started at 2 am. This child would be born at home with a mid-wife. I wanted a family centered experience and it was by far the best for me. Only 3 ½, hours with a warm shower during, and my good friend Judy preparing breakfast for my intense appetite after delivery, made for our 4th son, Christian's birth a very encompassing atmosphere. Breakfast over, the visitations began. Neighbors, siblings, parents. All the circumstances, of moving and birth, served to take me deeper into trusting the Lord. Being willing to take risks to find out He could work things out for good. We never did move…to a new home.

The church move we made a year prior already required a lot of change, but meeting many wonderful families, added to our ever-growing community. Nothing seemed as real and rich as the first small group when I first believed, if only because the lessons of faith I was learning held increased responsibility, a normal effect of maturing. Brad was now settled and communicating by phone weekly, deepening our conversations, easing my desire to have him back home. The interweaving of soul and spirit when the change of proximity requires adjustments can be difficult to navigate alone, but with Christ by my side and a total surrender of trust, I was seeing the benefits. Our childhood had great memories of time spent together. Our neighborhood was full of afterschool games, sledding, basketball, tetherball, kick the can, and more. Not one afternoon went by that we didn't need to be called home for dinner by the big "school bell" my mother rang when it was time for eats. Teenage years divided us. Raging hormones and competitive nature, kept us moving apart. I was very aware of my parent's support in my brother's sports activities and keenly aware that they weren't at mine. Cheering, track and basketball. I felt neglected and it pushed me into negative behavior patterns of rebellion. But rebellion would eventually take me so low that all I could do was look up. Then it was time to draw closer again with a new frame of reference, and maturity. Our friendship became a fulfillment of needed family acceptance and encouragement for both of us as a conversation over lunch gave way to the realization that we had both felt exactly the same growing up. We each thought the other to be the favored one.

Christmas came and so did Brad, visiting the family for Christmas. Opening the front door to receive one of his bear hugs is a memory that transports me back to the moment every time I think of it. The fun uncle, frolicking on the floor, making elephant sounds, tickles and giggles, and love to go around was endearing. His humor was timely, and contagious, and always welcomed at family gatherings. I was grateful to have him in our life.

The following year he remarried, and invited Ben for a lengthy stay that summer. Ben was happy to experience working landscaping, and the sights and activities of Southern Cali., returning the following year as well when he experienced a large 7.4 earthquake, Knotts Berry Farm and A Major League Padre's baseball game, along with being mentored to become a man. My brother was a good role model; his support was invaluable. Extending it to us again, when we found a house not far from our current one and located on the border of Dad's Farm/Mountain. Not unlike the NJ home, Dad's property afforded lots of place for activity. Family times spent there included fishing, camping, ice skating and roasting marshmallows and hotdogs on a fire and making fresh pine wreaths at Christmastime. The house we found needed love. Mom voiced her dismay at the work required. Not understanding how we could possibly want to move to a place that would take lots of renovation and effort. But I knew if it was God's will His specialty is taking broken things to restoration. A profound quote by Ann Voskamp in her book "The Broken Way" and her husband, Farmer Voskamp is painted on my living room wall and exemplifies my own feelings. "The seed breaks to give us the Wheat. The soil breaks to give us the crop, the sky breaks to give us the rain, the wheat break to give us the bread. And the bread breaks to give us the feast. There was once even an alabaster jar that was broken to give Him all the glory." —Ann Vaskamp "Never be afraid of being a broken thing." —Farmer Vaskamp Brad saw the vision for it. Auction results would tell if we would realize the vision. Plans for renovation and temporary accommodations of tent and garage during summer would enable repairs before cool weather arrived. Buyer secured, now all we need was to win the bid. Unfortunately, the buyer backed out and plans and dreams had to be shelved. Would we still love the Lord in the face of this closed door? Indeed, for he had not let us down, He knew where he wanted us, and we would grow where He had planted us on the very same mountain just 4 miles away.

Trusting for provision was tough, when groceries and finances were lacking at times, the blessing of the words of Psalm 126 NIV brought me peace.

> Restore our fortunes O'Lord
> Like streams of the Negev
> Those who sow in tears
> Will reap with songs of joy
> He who goes out weeping
> Carrying seed to sow
> Will return with songs of joy
> Carrying sheaves with him.

The new place of maturity brought more gladness of heart; using the word against worry and fear. 2 Chronicles says, joy and strength are in His dwelling place, I would endeavor to remain in His dwelling. The struggle was lessening.

CHAPTER 6 🌿

Removing the Thorns

And after you have suffered a little while the God of all grace
[who imparts all blessing and favor], who has called you to
His [own] eternal glory in Christ Jesus, will Himself complete
and make you what you our to be, establish and ground you
securely and strengthen and settle you.

1 Peter 5:10 AMP

September 1992, in a rare time when my thoughts were stilled,
I heard and recorded these words from the Lord.

"I am going to take you to a new place where you will have to
depend on me as never before, but you will also have more grace
the you have ever known. This will be a place of difficulty and
enormous blessing. You will come before me and I will enable you
to go through the storm. You have been faithful but need to prove
more persistent and consistent in our times together." His words
in Habakkuk, especially, 3:17-18 reminded me that no matter the
circumstance, "yet I will rejoice in the Lord, I will be joyful in God
my Savior." And the chapter of Jeremiah 6 reminded me of my
calling.

Confirmed when I received a prophetic word from someone, who could only know by hearing God, was a turning point. Difficult times were ahead but my confidence was in His words to me. Grace would take me through, and I would remember that whatever was coming, His grace is enough help.

Not many days passed this Word, Labor Day plans to celebrate a sister-in -laws birthday in upstate PA were in place. Gary's whole family would be there. Not only was there a birthday, but two anniversaries, one of which I was not aware. Suggesting that we celebrate the one anniversary I knew about, when we are out to eat on Friday evening, the news of my suggestion spread through the family "grapevine" stirring a "hornet's nest" of anger and assumptions.

The culmination of years of pent up family emotion and distorted perspective released a firestorm of anger during that weekend. There were birthday plans for one sister-in-law and two wedding anniversaries as well. A long weekend of camping on family property, dinner out, and a birthday BBQ were planned. On Sunday, I planned to return home with Ben to attend a family reunion with relatives visiting from California, via a ride with a family member leaving earlier than most.

My cousin and I hadn't seen each other since 1966 and now both married with children, were excited for the following day at Hershey Park. My ride home was discussed and decided upon. Sunday arrived with many tensions among the family. Erupting in a ruckus of anger and harsh words spilling into the atmosphere, everyone was involved. Emotionally charged, each person had a notion of what was going on in the fragmented scenarios in the house, outside: front yard, back yard, garage, and down the road at one brother's cabin. The whole picture was only available from one perspective. God's.

As words continued to heighten intensely, I had had all I could take. I was not going to allow abuse to beat me or my children into submission and a heightened emotionally charged atmosphere is the brainchild of the devil for hurt and pain with no concern for anyone's best interest. Gary and I had agreed on care for the other children resting with him and returning on Monday. Unraveling of the mounting tensions was triggered, Ben announced to me that others were irritated questioning him in anger about my leaving Gary with the children.

Ben was twelve years old and had no part in the decision and No one had talked to either of Gary or I about their upset. So, I addressed it. Within moments Gary averted another physical attack by stepping in between me and a family member. That member was going for reinforcement and headed down the road. Gary wanting to avert any more drama followed them in hope of peaceful resolution, but any hope of a civilized calm resolve went up in smoke and the fire of anger resulted in an inferno of fury.

Name calling, physical abuse to one of my children, subjecting children to trauma as again they witnessed out of control adults. My movement toward gathering my children to leave, moving toward the door with all children, but one, accounted for and by my side, trying desperately to remove us from the warzone. A furious brother-in-law came through the door grabbing my unaccounted for child, picking him up by the collar and slamming him into the wall, then racing toward me calling me an name I will not repeat, and hating that I did not fall at his words but forcefully and vocally spoke. "I am not a …and you need to move out of my way! We are leaving."

Out the door with all children, I called Gary who was down at the garage with another family member, trying as he might to put out a side fire, to tell him we were packing up. Fast and chaotically throwing our belongings into our wagon and getting the children, who were frightened and crying deeply, belted in.

In a few calm moments after the initial storm, I thought to thank my sister-in-law for preparations. Walking to the door of the kitchen, I came face to face with another brother-in-law who had come up the road just to get involved. His nasty words in an authoritative furious tone let me know there was not going to be a thank you or any discussion of resolve. Again, my inner strength rose to deny his vile name calling and accusations, that I should "get a job". He was met with my inner resolve to overcome his out of control emotions. While Gary was still trying to be the peace maker and put out another violent outburst in the front yard started by the same brother-in-law, who was now infuriated that his "authority" had been denied. Turning quickly from me to find someone else as a target for his angry bludgeoning words. I had children to calm. I waited in the car.

At this point, another approached to tell me that "None of this would have happened if it weren't for you!" I strongly replied that I would take responsibility for myself and my children but not for the actions of the others who were out of control with abusive behavior, at which point they also left me alone. Gary had no success in bringing complete peace. That day healthy boundaries would need to be well thought out to be put in place which would prevent any future violent scenarios.

The devastation of that day still has implications; yet unresolved, because the fragments of years past have not been pieced together. Family members too young or not present are left to draw unlikely conclusions and hold unforgiveness, preventing the healing of Jesus. But I can say, I see movement towards that end. The unraveling of events takes desire to know the cause and resolve the pain buried deep in the souls of people.

The roots of these character traits manifested that day is laid out in the scripture in James 4:1-2 states "What leads to strife (discord and feuds) and how do conflicts (quarrels and fighting) originate among you? Do they not arise from your sensual desires that are ever warring in your bodily members? 2 You are jealous and covet (what others have) and your desires go unfulfilled; (so you become murderers) (to hate is to murder as far as you hearts are concerned.) You burn with envy and anger and are not able to obtain (the gratification, the contentment, and the happiness you seek), so you fight and war. You do not have, because you do not ask.

I had started 12 years ago to be aware of my own attachments to the world and their effects in my soul and how they caused conflicts. I believe to this day that God wanted to reveal and free me from the attachments of the "world" of the family I married into. He broke us free, some of us from years of abusiveness, so that healing could begin. I was mature enough not to dwell in the circumstances of that day and to seek God for revelation of his intent. Letting go of abuse requires circumstances that put us in circumstances, over and above, our ability to control. That is when we realize our need for God to enter in and bring peace in the storm.

Not one person would escape untouched by hurtful words and actions. Opinions, hierarchical structures, violent suppressed anger, physical and verbal abuse all appeared that weekend. At the pinnacle of the explosion, Gary and I hastily packed and left before more violence leading to emotional trauma was unleashed in a family meeting, we chose not to attend because of heightened emotions. Endured names, accusations, physical abuse, I wish not to implicate or repeat, our family cried from the trauma of intensity. Consequences and severed relationships remain undiscussed and levels of unknown abuse happening to my own children over the previous years only came out into the open 20 years later. Of course, we have forgiven and had contact, but there are still those who may never choose to look at the consequences of that awful weekend or the behavior which caused it.

Following, a few weeks later, a call from the school nurse summoned me to the ER, as Aaron who was now in second grade, suffered a seizure. Shaken and disturbed, I would go before the Lord imploring His insight and wisdom. The Storm was building in strength, but I remembered his promise of grace to get me through if I would seek his presence. As a mother we struggle when our precious children suffer with no answers for the present. Our emotions go crazy with worry and fear. However, after seeking God, I had a sense that the reason for this seizure was not a physical one but spiritual. God would reveal what I needed to know after a couple of months. Medication seemed to control them, but I was not satisfied because of what I thought God was saying.

The beginning of December I mentioned to Gary that I thought maybe it was a good time to expose the children to a viewing and funeral before it happened to someone very important to them. Opportunity came when a dear uncle of mine passed opening the door for this experience. We took them and it went well. December would be a climactic month filled with surprises.

In preparation for the celebration of Christmas, the women of our fellowship rented the kitchen at the local Christian Day School and baked loads of delicious cookies to share. I loved making a German wreath cookie called Berliner Kranz, orange butter dough, topped with whipped egg white, green crystal sugars and red cinnamon candies. Christmas was a big celebration in our house growing up and my mom made it very special, with great food and lots of gifts. Celebrating changed for me with the focus on Jesus first, as his coming as a babe meant "Emmanuel", God with us. Worship was first on the list of activities on Christmas day. It was the day of baking though that opened the door to share my sensing for Aaron and what had been happening. Sharing burdens is very important, we can glean the fruits of the Holy Spirit, to help us. Bearing one another's burdens makes the difficult times easier. Prayers, wisdom, comfort, insights… which is what happened. One sister said to me while baking "You need to call Mark.". "Who is Mark?", I responded inquisitively. "He is a prophet." This was new to my experience and I wanted to understand. Preceding to tell me that he was part of our fellowship, living locally, and a phone call to him would be of great benefit to finding answers. These were the days of paying for each individual long-distance call and since I was in his locality, making the call from the school was profitable and timely.

Dialing his number and finding him at home was my first miracle. I told him who I was and how I came to call him. Going on to share the past few months with Aaron and the sensing about the cause of his seizures, in a moment of pause he interjected. "Did your father ever hand his business over to an evil man?" Immediately, my mouth dropped open in shock. "How did you know?" "God just told me." stated matter of fact with a sureness. Continuing, "This man bought curses on your family, one of which is the cause of Aaron's seizures." This aspect of God's wisdom and understanding revealed was one encounter I will never forget. It left me amazed and relieved having received confirmation of my own sense of spiritual understanding. Conversation continued.

Mark wanted to get together with us, Gary, myself and Aaron, only two days into the future. The date was December 17, 1992. A trip to his home began with a couple of hours of conversation and then prayer and agreement to break the curse by the application of the word of God and Jesus blood sacrifice. He led Gary and I to renew our covenant with one another because of spoken words of possible divorce and then prayed with us over Aaron. By the end of the evening we had peace that God was going to deliver Aaron and that our path had been cleared a little more closely to seeing God's plan for us. However, our involvement in Mark's ministry to us would continue with his request to honor God's desire to meet with me personally the following Monday as Mark heard God say He had work to do in me. Even as he made the request, fear began to speak about not doing the next meeting, but Mark addressed it telling me that I had nothing to fear. "Greater is He that is in you than he that is in the world." I John 4:4 was the word he quoted, followed by "God wants to move mightily on your behalf". Also using Romans 9:15, I will have mercy on whom I have mercy, and I will have compassion on whom I will have compassion. The day was set, Monday December 21, at 9 am. Our pastors would be there and close friends to offer their prayer support.

From the time we left Mark's house, the onslaught of the enemy was evident. He did not want me to keep the appointment. Negative thoughts flooded into my path, but discipline would help me, fear was trying to put a stop to this divine encounter. When it wasn't enough, I called Mark for reassurance. His words from scripture, "Greater is He that is in you, than he that is in the World." They were the weapon I needed to make it to Monday morning. I woke up to a sick child, but my fortitude resolved the attack, telling the devil that would not keep me home. Gary was going to meet me at Mark's and I drove the path of the unknown grace of God.

Arriving on time and somewhat anxious, Mark unfolded my life in questioning. Answers gave him insight into the strongholds the enemy had gained and ground in my soul still held in bondage. Three hours passed as my life unfolded in that room, prayers were being lifted continually, and Mark discerned it was time for all but Gary and I to leave. Mark ask me to stand before him and began to pray. Within moments his hand touched my forehead and God's power weakened me to drop to the floor. He didn't push and I hadn't resisted. Fully cognizant, the prayers and communication continued until Mark dismissed Gary with the words, "You can go now, things are going to get ugly." Lying on the floor, God revealed strongholds of which only I knew through Mark. My body felt many things, one of which was a force of electrical current so strong that many men would not have succeeded in lifting me up. Responding with God's words I declared my loyalty and commitment to Jesus. "Satan, I am no longer yours, I belong to Christ. I will serve Him and Him only. I will defeat you by His blood and my testimony. He whom the son sets free is free indeed. (John 8:36). I am washed and cleansed by the blood of Jesus. In the shape of the cross, my hands and arms felt the grip of the enemy and showed my hands to be gnarled and tense. My mid- section felt as if there were a ton of cement block weighting me down. I commanded the enemy to leave by the authority of Christ and the blood He had shed for the forgiveness of sins. Every enemy had to go. God's was delivering me for obedience and redemption, moving me into my next realm of authority for fighting the good fight. It was unexpected and amazing, nothing I could have imagined on my own. Battling another two hours, hands gnarled and the ability to feel the grip of the enemies claws hanging on and finally letting go, as I declared my identity in Christ and my resolve to fight the devil for the ground he had stolen, until Mark sensed the battle was done. Resting and abiding on the floor, worship music played, and I relished the freedom and euphoria of God's presence. Mark took a short break to eat, since he had fasted to ensure God within full strength. He returned to anoint me, bringing Shirley, a prophetess and mother in the Lord to join us. There was still more work to be done.

Death, Suicide, and Jezebel did not want to leave but more confession with declaration of desire to serve God overpowered them. Death and suicide left after some declaration and as for Jezebel, God gave instruction to go to my natural father, whom I had manipulated, looking for favor, and asking forgiveness for my wicked behavior. What Mark revealed was that I had had my father's favor all my life. I did not have to try to get it. Returning home to my father that very afternoon, fulfilled the anointing I had received to run to my Father/father quickly. Asking his forgiveness and receiving it opened the way for God to speak through me to command with authority that Jezebel to leave, which was realized the following morning when I awaken in total weakness and recognition of that spirit's presence. I crawled on my knees to the next room to find Gary, imploring him to pray in agreement that it would leave for good. Our prayers lifted and in a moment my strength returned. The battle to remain free was only beginning.

Now the 22nd, the Christmas preparations were in full swing, including children's school programs, last minute shopping for food and gifts, and last but not least another attack on Aaron taking me to the ER, but none the less armed with freedom for our welfare. Recognizing counter attacks, lead me to rebuke the spirits by name using the blood of Jesus and the Word as my weapons. My house was protected and a safe haven giving peace amidst the storm. This battle was greater but the similarity to the battle over my health ten years earlier was recognizable. I had learned the tactics of battling the devil, and praised God for his loving mercy and compassion and training, when a breakthrough to peace came on Wednesday. I had been asking the Lord when I would see it. That evening I would…materialism had pervaded my existence growing up. I never wanted for anything and that is not a bad thing in itself, however my source was my earthly father, not my heavenly one and that needed to change. For the first time ever in my life, I was able to walk through a store and not hear things like "look at me, buy me, I could use this," I realized a freedom to choose that had not been present in the noisy voice of the spirit of materialism the world promotes. God will provide all my needs according to his riches in glory. Philippians 4: 19 Amp reads "And my God will liberally supply (fill to the full) your every need according to His riches in glory in Christ Jesus." And backing it up is 2 Corinthians 9: 10 -11, Amp., And [God Who provides seed for the sower and bread for eating will also provide and multiply you [resources for} sowing and increase the fruits of our righteousness [which manifests itself in active goodness, kindness, and charity]. 11. Thus you will be enriched in all things and in every way, so that you can be generous, and [your generosity as it is] administered by us will bring forth thanksgiving to God.

Only two days, until our celebration and it was looking to be a glorious one filled with thanksgiving to God for all his generosity in Christ's provision of sacrifice. On January 1, I wrote this reflection in my journal.

> A time of humbling and losses.
> Good losses- those of God's will.
> Laying aside my will.
> Delivered by the mighty hand of God.
>
> Free to be led, as the Spirit of the Living God,
> sees purposeful.
> A time of learning again-
> A babe of the new wine.
>
> Oh Lord, lead me in this new year,
> In the way everlasting.

Keep me humble and do not allow me
To take any glory for myself.

I want to glorify your Name, Lord Jesus.
Walking in the Spirit.
Setting captives free.

Praying for my family, according to your word.
Your promise to restore the years the locusts have eaten.
My husband rising to leader of our home.
United in vision and purpose in the firm foundation Of your
Word, and the rock of revelation in Christ Jesus.

From mountaintop to valley, this is the journey of a solider in
the Kingdom of Almighty God's army. January 4th I was taken to
the Valley of death once again. What seemed like an ordinary day,
dinner with a brother and daughter, a Full-Gospel businessmen's
meeting for Gary and Chris, while Barbara and I remained
home after dinner, quickly changed after answering a call from
my sister-in-law from California. At 8:30 pm I heard the words
that would rock my foundation and my soul. A phone call from
Stephanie, Brad's wife. She was clear in her words. "Brad is gone."
What do you mean? "He died at 1 pm today." Further explanation
reveals the detail. He was struck at the job site just after returning
from lunch by a car that ran a stop sign, while the husband and
estranged wife were engaged in an argument with their three
grandchildren in the back seat, and went over the median to hit
him from behind. Impact broke his neck and he was pronounced
dead upon arrival at Orange County Hospital. There was nothing
they could do. She requested amidst the excruciating tears of grief,

"Your dad is not home, and I need you to go and be with your mom until we can reach him to go home to her." I immediately said I would, leaving our conversation until later. My whole being was in a mode I had never experienced. All at once shocked, grieved, and needing to act. A deeper loss than I wanted to believe.

Disbelief overwhelmed me and yet I said "ok and immediately gathered my things amidst tears (my own and the children's) drove in devastation of loss to my dear mother who needed my support. Instructions to Barbara to pray and read a bible story with the children were given. Halfway to my mom, I was seeking God, I heard a clear voice, "Your brother shall be as Lazarus." This was not an impression. My heart wanted to know the intimate details of this word. I felt His hope and love speaking to me. Whatever could this entail? Keeping it to myself for the time being and offering myself to my family as best I knew how during this difficult time of loss was my intention. Brad was only 36 and was to become a first-time father. He was the only of my brothers with whom I had close relationship. Why did this happen? It all seemed wrong but God knew and I was going to seek Him. He would have the answer. Brad would be buried here in our hometown, flown into PA and prepared by his best friend and funeral director, Steve. The family met with our pastor and made the plans. Who wanted to speak, hymns to be sung etc.; all the details that help us get through to the other side of burial? "Almighty Fortress is Our God" was a sure pick for singing as it exalts God in His sovereignty. I volunteered to do the eulogy. I would be honored to have a last opportunity to give my brother words so deserving of his life. After all, we were close and loved each other well, our friendship was certain. Early in the week of the funeral, it was midnight, overwhelmed with emotional sorrow, I sat in the kitchen to pen the words that God would give me to honor my brother and friend. Inspired by Holy Spirit, I wrote with no stopping and no redrafts. With words inspired by the Holy Spirit to plant, and honor both God and Brad, my eulogy was complete. Now the waiting, filled with hours of repetitive tears, hugs, and words of remembrance in the five days with family before the funeral. There was a service in California on Thursday, and he was flown home. Stephanie, and Jeff a close cousin arrived that night. Stephanie and Brad had announced only six weeks prior that they were expecting the arrival of a baby the following August. She would need extra care and God's great grace to carry this child under such extreme circumstance. She was surrounded by love.

Six hundred people poured out their love and support on Friday evening at the viewing. As usual everyone was relaying their stories and expressing personal grief over this tragedy. Sleep, a premium that week, may have been little, but God's presence energized us during this duration after which we returned home at 11 pm with imminent return by 9 am. Fear of standing before a full house had no place; my confidence in the words I received was sure.

Freedom had been given to the pastor to choose the scripture readings. He spoke and I wanted to go ballistic with joy and amazement. Beginning with John 11:1-12 "Now a man named Lazarus…" God was confirming his word to me! It took all the self-control I had not to jump out of the pew and shout "Hallelujah"! My body was tingling with the Holy Spirit. The eulogy would be next. Stepping up in boldness, words on the pages flowed with love and compassion for who God had given us in Brad. Joy and unity of faith affirmed Brad's life as purposeful and eternal. Our dear aunt wrote that the message of his life was well received, as many had spoken, and were moved to tears. I was pleased and assured that God used me to bless those in attendance.

Gathering that evening in my parent's home following a fellowship meal including Brad's favorite foods of Fig Newtons, and Wege's pretzels, the Holy Spirit visited and moved me to go to a secluded place, allowing me to discern his visit. Would it be now that Brad was to be resurrected? I only knew he was asking me to go to the cemetery at that time. The darkness was all around, and emotion stirred. Bowing down, I humbly ask the Lord to show forth his glory. I was scared of all the circumstance but waited for His direction. Entreating His will be done and decreeing that Brad come forth from the dead in the name of Jesus. Being still. Then His voice spoke. "You may leave now. I wanted to see if you would obey, so when the time comes, I know you will do as I ask." This would not be my last time of obedience in this matter. And again, God would speak. "Go in peace. I will do what I say I will do."

Many times, I doubted and was tempted to disbelieve the experiences. However, each time as I lay it before the Lord, His confirmation of what I heard would come. Two prophets in particular spoke, Dr. Bill Hamon and Kim Clement. Dr. Hamon in his book, Prophets and Personal Prophecy, writes of the history of the church and its foundations recorded in Hebrews 6.

"Therefore let us leave the elementary teachings about Christ and go on to maturity, not laying again the foundation of repentance from acts that lead to death and of faith in God, instruction about baptisms, the laying on of hands, and the resurrection of the dead, and eternal judgement." His book laid

out the previous restoration of these foundations in major moves
of the Holy Spirit beginning in the 1500's with Martin Luther
and the doctrine of faith in Christ and His grace, saying that all
would be restored including the resurrection of the dead before the
return of Christ.

Over and over in other manner of confirmation, God was
affirming. What I did not understand was His timing, causing
me to cast the "pearl" of my vision before people who would not
believe. Mockery, laughter, derision, and hope deferred caused
unbelief of my "own, but God in his mercy would teach me
wisdom and timing. God lives in time eternal; it is circular. Chuck
Pierce explains it this way. "Time is not Linear the way we think.
Time is in the form of a circle. Therefore, if we move toward our
future, God will restore our past." God is restoring my past. I
know this as reality. I will wait on Him for as long as it takes. He is
faithful.

CHAPTER 7

Everything's Coming Up Roses

We're just beginning and there's no stopping us this time.
—Everything's Coming Up Roses. 1959 Gypsy Soundtrack

It has been 25 years since Brad went home and 60 Years have passed since the writing of this song. 60 in God's kingdom is a significant number. Sixty literally means to heap or support, like a pillar with three beams in Hebrew. Father, Son, and Holy Spirit. The words speak of fullness. "You'll be swell! You'll be great! Gonna have the whole world on a plate! Starting here, starting now, Honey, everything's coming up Roses. Beginning and overcoming were the theme that resounded in the next season of my life. The previous season of difficulty played out just as God had spoken. Difficult but followed by enormous blessing. I was ready. I wanted the reality of 1 Peter 5: 10: …the God of all grace[who imparts all blessing and favor], who has called you to His [own] eternal glory in Christ Jesus, will Himself complete and make you what you ought to be, establish and ground you securely and strengthen and settle you.

1993 was the beginning of new adventures and new relationships. Shirley became a spiritual mother to me, and I became a spiritual mother to Leslie and Tracy. They were part of our fellowship and had gone to the same school. Personality wise they couldn't have been more different, except for the one factor we all have, human sin.

Leslie came into my life first, through a game night which put us on the same team. She was very intelligent and not to be taken for "retarded" something she said people often voice and an assumption used in my generation for anyone thought to be slow in learning. Leslie was born with Cerebral Palsy and suffered the misguided perceptions of people who did not take the time to know her. She needed love from people not condemnation. Amazed at her responses on game night she brought the team victory. We connected that night. I had learned in my college experience that most who are afflicted with cerebral palsy are very intelligent and Leslie was no exception. Leslie later introduced me to Tracy.

Our relationship formed solidly when she inquired at church about someone to do part-time care for her two young children. That person gave her my name. Working part-time and expecting a third baby in a few months we lived in the same county on opposite ends with her job in the middle. Our conversations built in duration when she picked the children up. She had a difficult upbringing, lacking parental involvement, and alcoholism. I knew this was a God appointed relationship when I found out she lived on Rosebud Road.

A fiery curly tousled red head, full of life and energy, who loved sports because she wanted to make her father proud. Tough and independent, due to circumstance, God watched over her and found in her a desire for salvation and growth at the young age of 15. Loving and knowing God is what the bible defines as eternal life in John 17:3. Tracy wanted this life.

Tracy quickly surmised my "open door" hospitality and availed herself to it often. A challenge to my flexibility and readiness to serve the Lord in season and out of season. Discipleship is a calling from Christ to each believer. Go and make disciples. Not converts. By inviting young believers to share in our everyday lives, we teach by word and example. Roses love food and water, pruning and cutting. They flourish under good caring hearts. Jesus talks about this. James 2:16 in The Contemporary Version puts it like this. "you shouldn't just say "I hope all goes well for you. I hope you will be warm and have plenty to eat." What good is it to say this, unless you do something to help." Convenience was not a consideration, learning boundaries though was a lesson to be heeded and task to be accomplished by all who would serve Jesus. The boundary lesson would continue building throughout time. Grace, grace and more grace to learn respect for others, give and take, for the good of all.

Leslie also needed boundaries. She was not afforded the freedom of dropping in anytime she wanted to visit, and her mode of visitation and teaching was the telephone. When jealousy and anger decided to use her emotion, calls with immediate hang-up were sometimes 15 times a day. My grace was not that mature and neither do I think it should be. I needed her to respect my time. Rearing five little ones and running a household was stressful yet 15 annoyance calls a day sometimes pushed me over the limit of my grace.

Only three years before, I became aware of my own lack of boundaries that allowed abusive ways to manifest in my life. Bold Love, a book by Dan Allander, gave me courage to look at this need in my life. Bold was a quality I had, but it needed tempered under the Lord's care. Many have asked me to pray that they too could have my boldness to which I freely honored their request. Love was something I don't recall knowing in the depths of my heart as a child. Mostly an emotion and often just a distant thought, I would have to learn to Love the way Christ did and Dan Allander helped a lot with understanding the "how to" of this virtue. Tracy and Leslie were God's intended vessels for my training.

Tracy became a true disciple of the Lord, sooner than Leslie. Three and a half years into my relationship with Leslie, frustration with progress, took me to my knees in prayer. Asking God for direction until he showed me that I was the mother bird and it was time to push her out of the nest. She would not learn to fly if she thought she could continually rely on me. The break came in a conversation relaying the answer I had received and then God spoke through me. Leslie, I am not doing anything that Jesus didn't do to his disciples. When …after 3 years, he left them and put them into the care of the Holy Spirit." The words flowed out of my mouth and I wondered where they came from. Certainly not my brain.

My afterthought marveled at the profoundness of His words. Under the care and surrender to the Holy Spirit, God will speak, and you will be amazed at the wisdom that comes forth. I really didn't think those words they just came out. I trusted God to care for her. Making tough choices in obedience can have harsh consequences when others only see part of the story. Christ sees everything: we can count on him for an answer that is best for all.

Tracy however, continued to grow, coming often to pray, read the word, talk, learn housekeeping skills at both our homes, child discipline and care, cooking, baking, loving, discussing, hugging, fellowshipping, more loving and sometimes we butted heads. That does not surprise me! Light has nothing in common with darkness. Jesus calls all disciples out of the darkness into the light.

I knew God was up to something good when Tracy would ask her most memorable question. "I have a question for you." It indicated she had been thinking deeply and wanted more understanding. Kitchen time was often truth time, and one evening as she dried dishes, it was truth in love talk. Glancing over at her hands, she had wrapped the tea towel, twisting it around one hand and holding it tightly with the other. "What are you doing with the towel? I queried. Her face and neck flushed red, her reply, "I am trying to keep from punching you in the face!" We laughed, knowing she was managing her anger and receiving the truth that could set her free. I trusted our growth together would make us Christlike and bring us successfully to our destiny. We would learn to love each other! It was part of his plan.

The plan included helping her become the wife and mother, God wanted. Teaching me to give His love to someone as deeply wounded as myself required His patience and grace. Her fiery temper evidenced itself a lot in our early years, but the more I continued sharing life; the power of his Love her heart softened so she could give and receive to the end of discipling others as well. We were a true match in passion. The happiness and joy of watching her unfurl was exhilarating and encouraging. We both wanted to quit at times but not at the same time, that way we could lift each other up. Even when she was on the edge, I gave her the choice to go or not. Telling her the consequence of losing our relationship, kept her on my staircase steps for two hours one evening until she made the decision to not give up. Her love for God and family, encouragement to forgive and love again kept her on the right path. The fruit of our mother daughter relationship was meeting our needs in all respects, spiritually, emotionally and physically.

Sometime, after seven years she asked me to accompany her to their family cabin a few hours away, for a girl's weekend. Spur of the moment timing required my flexibility but I sensed it was to be an important time. As the weekend unfolded, we knew the Lord had set apart this time for His work.

For starters, she heard my testimony for the first time. Imagine that! Most of the years were focused on Tracy's growth, so getting a few hours of sharing about Jesus work in me just hadn't happened. I shared God's work of love and forgiveness in my journey as she was held captive. Moments of surprise for her were preparing her heart for the work of Christ in her own life. God held her captive in the car for the duration of the trip.

His words and works became the catalyst for healing her woundedness. Sleep was minimal but non the less God energized us because that is what he gives when we need it to accomplish his will. Tracy had grown in her spiritual gifts, prophetic anointing, thoughtfulness, deep seeking. I benefited as well, reaping a friendship of understanding and respect. Her words and visions brought me life and encouragement: they were timely and appropriate. Our times of sharing were like family. Pretenses were non-existent in our relationship. We understood one another like no one before had in prior time. She had adopted my love of hospitality, opened her heart to other's needs, and ministered wherever she went in Jesus' name. It was time for her own advancement of authority and blessing.

The night was filled with God's presence in our conversation and He answered her questions. One about meeting needs within his will, coming to understand that we don't just do things without prayer. God always will impress upon us his desire continually. Sometimes the enemy tries to get us to give when it isn't appropriate, depleting our being and resources. When this happens, it is enablement. For example, you may see someone's need and try to meet it without seeking the Lord. The need they have is deeper than a material thing. God wants to meet the deeper need of deliverance for freedom's sake in that person, like Oswald Chambers proports in his words I wrote on page 99, Jesus must be first. Our humanness seeks people to meet our need but God is to be our provider. If we only meet the material need that person may come to think we are there source that will meet their needs, not God. Not that we shouldn't meet a material need if God says to do so, but prayer will differentiate the need. Tracy needed boundaries. God would help, but for now his focus was on her wounded heart and after a lengthy time of worship, and prayer, He laid her on the floor in the spirit and she felt his hand reach into her chest and pull her heart out to do spiritual surgery. She came away healed and in new perspective of her life and ministry.

After this weekend, our relationship transitioned. No longer mother-daughter only but also sister-sister. Maturity was coming and leading us in His new way. She was inspired to write me these words.

A Mother's Love
By Tracy DeHart
As the years have gone by,
A Mother's love goes deeper and deeper,
Into the heart of her children.

Even though she has said
"The rod is narrow and the path is straight."
What is a Mother's Love?

A love that comforts.
A love that prays,
Even when her children want to walk in their own ways.

Her words spoken:
Gentle, kind firm and sweet.
Wanting God's best even in the midst of trials.

In the years a child grows,
I've learned a Mother's love never ends.
It is not just for a time and a season
But for always.

A mother, walking in the ways of the Lord,
Is like a pure reflection;
Of God's love to His children…

It Never ends and NEVER dies.
As a child grow, it is like a rose…
They blossom…Then Bloom.

I want to thank my mother
For the love she has sown,
Because the mother, who has prayed, fed and watered me,
Has become my Best Friend.

Slowly, ever so slowly the "Rosebud" was opening. Our relationship had indeed transitioned. Sensing the Lord's instruction to step back in some ways in her life and go forward in others, so she could fully bloom under the Lord's care and nurture. She would open a business of sports cards and collectibles in her hometown and I would help with that endeavor.

Located on Main Street and set up in a very small historical building, originally a cigar shop. The vintage screen door opened to reveal original floors and windows, boasting display cases from the earlier times of the 20th century. Passers-by inquisitive to explore treasures became the focus of hours of ministry through conversation. My blessing was to use my retail, design and ministry skills, all while enjoying the sound of Amish buggy horses, clip clopping past the shop, the squeaking of the screen door opening and the history and aesthetics of beautiful collectible that survived many years.

Our families continued sharing holidays, school and church events, fellowship and family birthday celebrations. Then in her third year a new addition to her family changed the vision. The baby girl came prematurely taking Tracy to the hospital daily, a good hour's length of travel from home. Transition was inevitable. I loved the store and Tracy loved flea markets. On a weekly basis, she would survey the shelves and pack her picks for the flea market. At first, I didn't seem to mind, accompanying her many times, but the packing and unpacking just was not my "cup of tea". With her additional motherly responsibilities, store tasks fell on me to do all the unpacking and redisplay causing me displeasure.

I would take my frustration to God. He would help. I was overly concerned about addressing my feelings with Tracy and within weeks of praying she decided to close the store. Relief came on all counts. Her choice did bring more distance and less interaction between us. I moved back into the retail sector at the mall, while she continued flea markets and online selling. For 2 1/2 years this continued until in the Fall of 2006. She had been working in a plastics factory and called to share news of difficult nature.

A health concern was motivation to connect for prayer. The call was a chance to catch up on our lives. Significant news of a doctor visit had revealed a lump in her breast. Biopsy and surgery were schedule quickly and the removal of lymph nodes to be tested as well. Seeking the Lord's counsel and direction was guiding her away from traditional medicine in favor of alternative treatment.

Her research and nutritionist led her to Dr. Robert Rowan located, in of all places, Santa Rosa, CA. His skills in Insulin Potentiation Therapy, IPT, studied in Mexico with high success rates seemed the answer she was seeking. IPT works on the principal of a less toxic amount of chemotherapy using insulin to attract sugar loving cancer cells, causing them to open up, then quickly following the insulin with the 10% (90% less than U.S.

treatments) of chemotherapy. In conjunction, Detox therapies at a ministry center in proximity would also help to restore her body to a natural healthy state. A consultation was arranged for early in February.

Tracy needed a companion for the trip. Her right arm had been rendered useless for a while now and no one could give her any concrete reasons. A pinched nerve was the best offered. She began seeking the Lord as to who he would choose to accompany her. The Lord spoke. "Susan". She hesitated and returned to Him not wanting me to be the one and each time hearing my name. Now only ten days remained until the time of the departure. Her reticence would have to give way to courage and she finally ask me. My own courage lacking, I figured Gary's response would be the clincher in the final decision.

Overwhelmed at the prospects of trust needed to handle all the aspects of this seemingly huge responsibility. Flying to California, renting a car, a wheelchair, the list went on and on in my mind. But God…. Gary said yes, that she needed my support. Of course, she did. I could not abandon her now. We had been through so much together. God had intertwined our hearts with his and each other. Asking for God's confirmation, the process only took three days… now only a week until departure. Opening my email on that day, revealed a prophetic word from Catherine Brown on the Elijahlist website.

You could have blown me over with a puff of your breath as I read the title. "A Call to be Undone…The Rosebud becomes a Rose." "God's spirit is shaking our hearts to surrender to him." She continues, stating God is looking for face to face encounters with his children so that we might become so absorbed by His gaze of love that we will become undone.

"As I think of the year that lies ahead my heart has been captured afresh by Christ's love. We can do nothing apart from His love. His call to remain (John15) is a clarion message to the Church in this hour. Our best plans amount to nothing if they do not flow from hearts that are undone by His love. May we be increasingly captivated by Christ and experience His divine romance in order that we might bring our Heavenly Father much glory as we experience His joy. My prayer: "Undo me with your love Lord so I can love Tracy through this difficult time.""

Catherine goes on to speak of Isaiah's call from God, recorded in the book of his name in chapter 6 verses 1-9. Isaiah proclaimed he was "undone". Following she listed ways we may accidentally, maliciously, purposefully or even thoughtfully become undone. The last is the one I want to explore here. Reference was to a shoelace analogy, accidentally undone, or untying our shoe purposefully and thoughtfully. Undone of our own will. Possibly after a long and tiring day, to experience the glorious feeling of wiggling our toes and resting our feet. The fresh air is relaxing! This purposeful, thoughtful choice to be undone is a lovely experience with no fear, anxiety or harm in it. We freely choose to enter in, and the results are delightful.

Two paragraphs follow, unfolding the quote opening my Chapter 5., explaining God's tender care. He knows exactly how to usher us through the process of bud to full bloom. Forcing premature blooming might eliminate it, but God has His perfect timing. Looking at our hearts in a similar way we can see the comparison and consider our end. God wants, like he did with

Isaiah, to meet with us face to face becoming absorbed by His intent and purposeful look of love, to undo the same within us just like the rosebud. Experiencing God in this manner we are opened to revelation and impartation. His love will give us the ability for His mission, thus spilling over to others the goodness and grace we have there received. Her conclusion: "Such life changing encounters cause transformation in us that becomes a catalyst for divine transformation in the nations.

The encounters of this adventure would bring an assuredness of God's love for us as individuals, friends, sisters, the Church community and the non-believers whose lives with whom we would intertwine. From the moment we left, the air held expectation of answered prayers and provision, we knew nothing about, waiting in the wings of heaven to be loosed on our behalf. God was wanting to heal and reveal His greatness and all the blessings a trial of such paramount enormity could bring forth because we chose to worship Him despite difficulties.

Without doubt, transformation was sure, grace and mercy poured forth like rain in a dry summer season. Set to fly on February 3rd to Oakland, California, where an upgrade in our rental car, was already waiting. The compact version would have made it a struggle for Tracy's in and out, but the upgrade was a perfect height. Oakland to Santa Rosa (Saint Rose), lol, was beautiful and the weather sunny. The people we had met thus far were pleasant, making any lingering fear melt away. Anxiety of driving on a six-lane freeway was nowhere, as God had prepared me with driving in Philadelphia traffic the previous four years.

The inner knowing of my needed help, gave way to love and sacrifice, making me appear confident, calm, feeling strength

I didn't know I had within myself. I can do all things through Christ who strengthens me (Phil. 4:13) was alive and proving His truth.

The presence of God with us enfolded everything. Our approach into Santa Rosa was a fresh and welcoming road. Palm trees lining the boulevard, sunshine abounded and reminded Tracy of a prophetic dream of mine from the beginning of our relationship. In my prophetic dream, a white vacation house on the corner of crossroad, lined with Palm trees, was the location of my family and close friends. Evening had come, and the children settled in the second story bedrooms were sleeping soundly. Outside the sun had gone down but light was waning. The picture window in front of us, revealed the dusk. 9 p.m. approached and we were relaxing with conversation. The scenic views of palm trees waving in breezes suddenly changed. Winds were increasing in strength and the sky revealed the darkness of storm. Excusing myself, I wanted to check on the children upstairs. All was well. They were snug and sleeping soundly. Momentarily the scene from the rear of the house caught my attention, drawing me to linger in its view. Deep darkness was on the horizon and I spoke down the staircase. "It looks like an approaching tornado", then returning to watch in peace as it formed and came at quick speed right for us. My heart and emotions were at peace and had no fear of impending destruction or danger. Eventually, it came up to the house at which point I moved to the window closer to the road. Suddenly the tornado stopped moving forward but was still spinning. The voice of God spoke. I want you to see what is inside". The spinning ceased. In "Let's Make a Deal" fashion, two doors parted at the center, revealing a roaring inferno of flames and crackling noise. Loud and furious. I observed. "Ok you have seen enough." Immediately the doors closed and whirling forward the tornado took a sharp and exact right turn passing the front of our house, soon visible from the picture window once filled with calm vistas, now destroying everything. Palm tops were blown off their once firm foundation. The dream ended there, but its implications did not. This was only one of the applications it prophetically held in its details. We both agreed we were in that house and the storm would come.

Settling into our extended stay hotel with a kitchenette enable our long days and strict dietary requirements to be easeful. We would have Sunday to gain perspective and settle in comfortably before Monday's appointment with Dr. Rowan. Sunday, we explored our surroundings, seeking food and noticing another prophetic signpost just across the road from our hotel. "Journey's End" and another on the round barn beside us, reading "Fountain Grove." Curious what journey was ending, but assured that the fountain of God's love was in this place. Monday would come soon enough. For now, we enjoyed each moment for all the joy and pleasure we could exact.

Monday morning's ten-minute ride to Dr. Rowan gave me a sense of the impending tornado and sharing my thoughts with Tracy revealed a dream she had during the night before. The moment I spoke she saw us as "in the reality" of it. She had seen a tornado coming right for as we headed down the road to Dr. Rowan. Warning me in fear, pleading with me to get out of its path. In boldness, I responded, "We are not moving out of the way. We are going to go right through it." Little did we know the tornado of circumstance to follow in the coming days. But hindsight revealed that we did indeed "Go right through it."!

CHAPTER 8 🌿

Enjoying the Fragrance

Our Creator God knows exactly how and when to unfurl each
petal, ushering every bloom through the process of completely
closed to opening up under his tender hand to becoming a
thing of exquisite beauty that releases and reveals glorious
fragrance and become a joy to all who gaze upon it.

—Catherine Brown

For to God we are the fragrance of Christ among those who
are being saved and among those who are perishing.

—2Corinthians 2:15 Christian Standard Bible.

Our appointment that day revealed high toxicity and the
immediate implementation of needed protocol for her return to
health. 14-hour days of detoxification, and regimented nutritional
treatments. The offices of Doctor and Detox Ministry were within
the same complex and worked together for years. Karen the
head of Cleansing Ministries had evolved in skill when her own
husband needed health. He recovered under her care and she was
led by the Lord to do the same for others. Ruth was Karen's intern,
and both were committed believers of Jesus. By weeks end the
love of Christ was bonding us together, extending refreshment

and healing for all. Entering the infrared sauna, songs of praise rose in the steamy hot atmosphere, releasing not only toxins, but continued joy. Continuing with oxygen therapy on a tread mill, instead of the hyperbaric chamber, due to difficulty getting in and out, she put on an oxygen mask and walked. Oxygen rich environment is essential to health. Somedays I walked with her or read scripture aloud to undergird and build up our strength to continue each day. Karen and Ruth joined in as afforded by their schedule. Other days, I took my walk outside in the community. From 8 a.m. -noon the variety of therapies extended and grew our knowledge and health. Leaving, we walked to Dr. Rowan's office across the parking lot.

After getting situated, I returned to our room to make us lunch in our kitchenette. Dr. recommended, totally organic, 70% raw and 30% cooked. Quickly learning all our organic shopping options was a great benefit and my cooking skills learned from Grandma allowed for creativity of satisfying meals. Always, Tracy expressed appreciation for especially the warm cooked meal of the day. Mornings were always a nutritional raw fruit and vege shake made quickly after our morning showers and grooming. Grooming and care reinforced my love to Tracy who had grown up caring for herself. She loved the blow-dryer styling, lotions, and clean clothes I provided as well.

Wednesday was Tracy's 37th Birthday. Wanting specially to make her feel loved and special I included in our day blessings to help put the current trial on the back burner if only for a short time. It was this day she would get her pic line inserted to make treatment more streamline. Her arrival at the Dr.'s office was greeted with gladness and a bouquet of gorgeous fresh cut flowers.

The effect was welcomed, along with good food (minus cake) and presents and most of all well wishes and conversation with her family at home. The laundered new p.j.s and Joyce Meyer magazine finished the celebration surprises or so I thought.

Plumping pillows and getting comfortable in our beds, I read from the magazine aloud. Inspiration stirred questions which led to discussion and increased felt presence of the Lord with us. Revelation within Tracy continued until the wee hours of the morning when we finally stopped around 4 a.m. Holy Spirit was back, only a short time later when we awakened to begin our routine and was speaking and changing us throughout the next two sleep deprived nights, bringing with Him, repentance, healing, visions, fulfillment surrender and tears. The long-awaited result of all my years of ministry in her life, a realization of the love I had given to see her into the fullness of His grace and purpose for her life. A love she now was expressing as a hope for her own children. Seeds planted being harvested. Our Lord was speaking with us. Caring for us. Giving us peace amidst the storm.

Tracy had to battle the last night against the spirit that had plagued her life until Christ showed her the way to Him. Redemption drew nigh, as she declared victory and denied the enemy access forever. The breakthrough to freedom had come. She was experiencing the next level of freedom in the goodness of God's love and a healthiness she had not felt in a very long time.

Saturday morning was enveloped by joy. Arriving at detox with Karen and Ruth only added more joy as they understood and could visibly attest to what we proclaimed. Ruth described her encounters with us in a post card as Sweet friendship, filled with skill to be able to focus and stay inspired with another person. They showed radiance, fun, attentive respect and excellent devotion. Ruth came through the door and checked on Tracy's treadmill progress, exclaiming the decrease in time for the number of steps as close to two minutes less than the day before. Tracy extatically turned sideways toward her to acknowledge her and within moments I was catching her as she flew backward to my unsuspecting arms. I heard a crack coming from her left arm as I caught her and steadied her fall. Only the day before, she had gone for a Pet Scan and results were still out. Gratefully we thanked God that I had been there to break her fall. Tracy said there was no pain after in her arm and we observed no evidence of a break. Observation would continue for further symptoms.

More grace and strength. Requirements necessary to now take on added responsibility of total care, including feeding and personal care she had thus far done for herself. Always the strong and independent type, Tracy's physical incapacity, would give way to strengthening her interdependency on a spiritual level. Working together to give her character a much-needed increase of faith in God to get her through the test. She smiled despite all she faced and was flowing with love.

The following day was Sunday and a welcome invitation from Ruth came to join her house church group for worship. Both of us were asked to share our testimony of God's work, revealing how He was giving us his grace and provision. Hearts were touched and tears flowed. This time was uplifting for all and we were sent on our way with a great financial blessing to help with expenses. Our afternoon, we ogled at the Luther Burbank Gardens and enjoyed God's outdoor creations of flowers, cactus, and trees. The sun was shining and warm. Not the cold weather we had left behind at home.

Monday the circumstance of her condition would reveal stage four bone cancer from her neck area through her hips, but Dr. Rowan remained positive in his hope to heal her. She noted that her pic line was burning and determination after inspection gave no indication of infection. By Wednesday however, the arm became hot and swollen. A nearby hospital agreed to do x-rays on Thursday night, hoping this would rule out a break. Grateful for their willingness to work with an alternative care doctor, we waited the late evening hours for results. I personally viewed the film and could see the undefined tissues and bone where there was supposed to be clarity. Reality was setting in she needed a miracle. Spent in every sense of the word after a 20-hour day, emotionally and physically, we arrived at the hotel at 1:30 a.m.

Sleeping in a little later than usual, Karen and Ruth had no idea yet of all that had taken place the day before. Filling them in on the details for prayer, following usual procedures, then off across the lot to Dr. Rowan. We were called into His office where we would face another paramount adventure in our journey. Since Monday's results of the Pet Scan, Dr. Rowan had been working on plans for her treatment, realizing the danger, of possible additional breaks including a spinal one, explain her need for more extensive care. Hospital San Martin, Tijuana, Mexico where Dr. Geronimo Rubio, a forerunner in cancer treatment, was consulted. She would be cared for by a competent staff of professionals in a twelve-bed hospital. It was desirable that I stay with her to support her, as all patients did better under these circumstances with familial or friend support. This would extend our time together another three weeks. Again, I would call Gary. Hoping he would say, "come home, you are needed here." He was firm in his reply that Tracy needed me now more than ever. I still tried to arrange for me to stay in the states just across the border with a relative. That was met with a negative. God was pointing me in the direction of Tijuana.

Dr. Rowan exerted emphatically the need for such treatment and His words were, do not pass go, do not collect $200, go straight to Tijuana. You need to arrive by Sunday noon at our office in Bonita, just before the border. Fortitude and Bravery, that's what I needed to face the whirlwind of preparation for the journey south of the border. 575 miles to go after collecting all Tracy's records from three hospitals, laundry and packing, mapping and to finish, an accident in the locale of our hotel left us without electricity until after 9 p.m. that evening. But God… had it under control. Our evening meal, at an unaffected Asian Restaurant, spoke loudly of the sacrifice to onlookers who voiced their observations of my dedication and love for one another, as they left. Everything worked out for our departure on Saturday morning.

Tracy voiced her own thoughts on the trip, and she recalled memories of a trip we had taken to Chicago, when she was the driver and I was anxious. This time though I would be driving, and she could observe God's maturing process that gave me peace. Simple understanding was needed; God's grace is enough, and we would trust Him again.

329 miles landed us in Bakersfield at about 10 p.m. Saturday on my Aunt Almeda's doorstep. Lovingly, in her own ministry to Christ, she lodged and fed us, providing a much-needed refuge

from the storm. A refreshing familiarity of lifelong love. Tracy found comfort on the recliner with ease of getting up and down. I slept nearby in the guestroom where I could hear her voice if she needed me. Morning came soon and we were sent on our way with more unexpected financial provision and food supply to feed us on our way. It seemed so much like Christ's command to his disciples to not take anything with them when they went out to minister. He was providing through His body, easing the burden.

At this point our route took us to the coast, allowing the scenic beauty of twirling windmills, sun-kissed shores, sky high mountains, vineyards bursting with grapes awaiting harvest to lighten our spirits and give us grateful hearts for all we were enjoying of God's majestic creation which is never boring and ever changing. Ramon would meet us in Bonita, where the landscape was filled with breathtaking flowering Birds of Paradise and take us to San Martin Hospital. His smile brought us comfort. And his servant attitude made the transition easy. We arrived at 3 p.m., getting quickly settled in before dinner to our two-bed suite. Meeting our new "family" assured us we were in good hands with all who worked to bring us care. Ministry would abound within the hospital walls.

Not without challenges of normal relational adjustments. Continuing to live by faith, we saw healing, salvation and answers to prayers. Starting with dearest Lisa, across the hall, who made herself known immediately. Traveling from Utah, a retired businesswomen and therapeutic nurse practitioner she was being treated for throat cancer, but non the less welcomed us enthusiastically. She was protective of us and stopped someone from entering our room while we were away. Sharing with her, opened the conversation to faith. She seemed to be a believer, and we enjoyed fellowship. She had nobody with her for support and we were happy to oblige, whatever she desired from us. She came to us on at least three occasions in our time of stay for prayer, one stating extreme pain in the throat area which we responded to by laying on of hands. God answered and touched her completely relieving it immediately. We rejoiced with her. Then later she told us that she had accidentally pulled out her port for medication while dressing. It had been about a week since it happened, and the nurses were unable to find a new vein for insertion of a new one. Limiting Lisa's treatments, she implored us to pray again. Specifically, she requested that they find a vein on the first try. Ask and you shall receive! All of us were blessed when God answered our prayer of agreement (Matthew 18:19).

Some time had passed after we established our friendship and Lisa said she had something she wanted me to read. Holy Spirit revealed to me that it was the book of Mormon, and when she approached me again to read it, I said "Do you believe Christ is Lord?" Affirming she did, I reassured her that was the foundation we would stand on together, providing a boundary of unity. She was able to bless me with her healing touch when my lower back and neck needed massage. Our relationship remained intact and continued after we left the hospital.

The staff including Dr. David Romo, Dr. Wendy, Dr. Caesar and Dr. Romero along with Guadalupe, Olga, Leanor, Paulina, Mario, Mary, Lucia and Cook were very pleasant and did all they could to see we were taken care of offering personal conversation and attentive observations. The beautiful pool area offered fresh lemons for water or fish and a place for sunshine. Dr. "David" was our advocate and helped greatly in Tracy's protocol.

Paulina loved Jesus too and was head nurse making sure the protocol was followed. She and most of the others followed Christ and believed and then one day Guadalupe asked if I could share with her the faith I had in Jesus. Excitedly we made time one evening by the poolside. I cut her hair, we talked of spiritual steps and she accepted Christ's gift of salvation in prayer. Joy filled the atmosphere.

Fellow patients and support providers opened doors to minister as well. Sherri and her mother were also from PA. Sherri was supporting her mother through uterine cancer treatments. A finance investor, she kept a PA time schedule, arising early in the morning to work via computer. One night a storm took the electrical power and rendered everything to darkness. Overly anxious about the possibility of not being able to get power restored, as the outlook seemed bleak. I left the conversation saying, "Don't worry, Tracy and I will pray now." Skeptical looks turned into belief when ten minutes later all power was restored. You may call it coincidence; I call it the work of a loving Father who wants to show his love to all, including the "doubting Thomas'.

Tracy was having trouble the first four days remaining in a good attitude. Fasting all food and receiving only organic carrot juice was not a familiar diet and she hated it. Carrots were not her favorite and no solid food made her "hangry". I did my best to lift her up and tell her she could do it. I knew fasting as a practice for spiritual growth and breakthrough during long seasons of test and trial, this was similar. My encouragement helped and she did make it through. I am happy to say. The journey thus far had been beneficial to both of us for reducing toxicity and weight. By the end of our time, I felt like I was walking on air and had downed my weight by 17lbs. I was refreshed and renewed, an expectation that I did not have at the outset.

Three weeks passed by quickly, health and spiritual growth advancing. The Master gardener was working his life into our unfurling, as his beautiful fragrant Roses. Many more are the testimonies received during this time. My journals lack through the period, for free time to do nothing a premium. Yet the few notes I had, reminded me of a generous Father who will gladly join in helping us through difficult circumstances upon our invitation. As we all journey, we may have forgotten this fact. But it is never to late to grow with him and participate in His plans for us and others. When we finally realize we are lost and the ONLY WAY is crying for His help, He WILL show up and super naturally change our lives for the good. We just need to recognize that crying out for His help is good and continue to do it always, because He wants to answer our calls.

The day of departure from our new family at San Martin arrived. Saying goodbye to all those who served us and the ones who also were suffering was a sweet sorrow. We had connected on so many levels and developed a great appreciation for each experience. But we also longed for home and the familiarity of family and friends. There were definity mixed feelings of joy and sadness. Tracy was greatly strengthened and still relishing the spiritual freedom she had gained. Neither of us knew what a jubilant adventure God had prepared, and it wasn't over yet. Returning to our car in Bonita, our goal was the distance back to my Aunt Almeda's for that day. I had hope not to be on the Los Angeles Freeway during Rush-hour but that didn't happen. Philadelphia traffic had not prepared me for that number of cars and lanes, but then again, stopping for dinner at P.F. Chang's could make the wait for it to pass very enjoyable. And shopping for outfits to return to PA even more so.

Back on the road before dark, Aunt Al received us about 10 p.m. Exhausted from the drive and ready to sleep, a cup of chamomile tea and a little fellowship ended with goodnight hugs and kisses. Tonight, Tracy wanted to share the king size guest bed. Ahhh…relaxed and snuggling into my covers, I was drifting off to sleep quickly but not before I heard…" Mom, I need to go to the bathroom." I think it was longer than I realized but groggily, trying to remain in sleep mode, we made our way to and from, happy to return to my warm, safe, comfy bed. I had tucked her back into bed and walked around the bed, climbing in, once again snuggling under the covers, and was almost asleep, when I heard her mumbling something. I thought "NOW What?" but waited and then quiet. It was too late to be having a conversation on my account and with that it was "Lights Out".

Waking up, I recalled her mumbling and questioned if she had been talking in her sleep. "No" was her emphatic response followed by "I saw something. Do you want to know what I saw? My curiosity was aroused. Responding with an affirmative and resounding "Yes", she started describing what she saw when we returned from the bathroom early that morning. A HUGE lion reclining in the middle of our bed. We entered the room and He graciously got up and walked off the bed, waiting until she was settled and I too. Then He climbed back up and lay down between us. The Lion of Judah was there with us, He is a symbol of Christ throughout the scriptures. One meaning is a strong fighter against the enemy. He was with us to protect and defend us. What an awesome experience to bolster our faith. Tracy was a little shaken at first but soon realized He meant no harm.

We left Aunt Al mid-morning, with the sun shining brightly and our spirits high. Driving to our final night in Oakland, we enjoyed more raw snacks enroute. I felt sometimes like the police, when Tracy so badly craved a snack that wasn't on her diet. So, when she asked me to get something out of the vending machine at the rest stop, I cajoled and asked, "Did you eat your veges?" "No", she said. Agreeing that if she ate her raw carrot quota, I would allow her one treat that we agreed upon. Still not having accomplished that requirement by rest stop, the treat of Doritos was tucked into my side compartment until finished. Whittling away nibble by nibble she thought when I wasn't looking, she could slyly let the carrot fly out her window. "Sly Boots" was observed. I did see. That broke our agreement. It seemed like a small thing to her, but to me it was big. An underlying deceptive attitude toward dishonesty. She was angry, seething quietly to herself as we headed up the coast. I told her to talk to God about it and see what he had to say. Her anger reminded me of my own on the couch, 20 something years before, but God did speak to her about respecting our agreement. She apologized and peace was restored. Our evening of room service, a movie and mani-pedi's was relaxing. Early to bed was preparation for a trip in the dark to catch our flight home. We were excited to be at "Journey's End" in another aspect. Journey's End was indeed a prophetic sign post, indicating much more than the entrance to a trailer park.

Our flight was attended by the Lion of Judah whom she saw laying in the aisle of our plane, majestic and beautiful, guarding us on our way. We touched down safely, emphatically greeted by Chris and the children and Gary. My family prepared an organic dinner. My children, parents, and husband welcomed me with love and appreciation, a " Welcome Home" banner, and deliciously prepared meal acknowledged my presence was missed. Tracy's arrival was unlike mine, thinking I had mentally prepared her family for meeting her needs, that was not at all received. Weeks following had nothing in resemblance to her care the prior five weeks.

Sadly, the distance between our homes and God's call for me to support her daily routine had ended and transferred back to her family, leaving her lacking. We did call one another for ministry and visit but my new full-time job which I had sought prior to the trip became a reality and no longer were my days totally at home. We missed each other; she penned these words.

"Mom, I know I have said thank you so many times, but I wanted to put on paper how God has changed our lives and our families in five weeks. I want to say how honored I am to have you as a mom. You taught me so much about me that it changed my life forever. I know my attitude was not always good, but you taught me to be thankful in the midst of it all Thank you for loving the Lord with all you heart and teaching me to do the same with NO COMPROMISE. Thank you for crying out to God to save my life. It was a turning point for me. I know you sacrificed a lot in five weeks for obedience in the Lord. I pick this card because it reminds me of what you enjoy. The Garden. And the teapot reminds me of all the hospitality moments we've shared. You are such a blessing and even though it took me fourteen years to know your love for me; it has changed my life FOREVER! Tracy

Three weeks later in April another visit to Dr. Rowan, a pet scan revealed significant improvement. Our hope for recovery was bolstered by the news. She also went back to San Martin Hospital another three times each time receiving similar treatment and loving care. She believed God had spoken total healing. In July, following one of her visits we planned a celebration for her with friends, but sadly she got sick and went to the local hospital. Our celebration turned prayer vigil. She had contacted E. coli virus and three weeks of fighting it left her weak and in respiratory failure, but not before I had the chance to reassure her of God's willingness to care for her and a word of scripture given to Gary to encourage her. She was frightened about leaving her five children. I wanted her to know that God knew everything, and he cared for them too. Necessity moved her to a larger medical facility. Her condition worsened as three more weeks passed. Visiting her after or before work hours, praying and wanting the best, trusting God for His outcome, left all of us who loved her wondering what was going to happen.

I loved her friendship, her thoughtful understanding of my own struggles, weaknesses, wounds and failures. Her smiles, laughter, and generosity and words of encouragement let me know she was a true friend. I hated seeing her go through the difficulty, but I also knew she had come to a very stable place in her relationship with God in her circumstances.

And so, the Rosebud became a Rose!

CHAPTER 9 ❧

American Beauty Rose

Awake, North Wind,

And come Southwind!

Blow on my Garden,

That its fragrance may spread abroad.

Let my beloved come into his garden and taste its choice fruits.

Song of Solomon 4:16

"For He loves each one of us, as though there were only
one to love."

—Hinds Feet on High Places

My own unfurling to full maturity still in progress but Tracy
received her healing in Heaven. September, she left this world,
and I suffered great loss. Time was of the essence to make the
transition out of grief and into full realization of all the effects and
results of our experience and her death. God was not finished with
me yet.

Amazing as it may seem, my journals revealed back in the 90's
that Tracy had actually seen herself going into a bright light. A
foretelling we did not perceive but non the less revealing after the
fact. About 6 weeks after her funeral, which had given me great

opportunity to share with many people the wonderful relationship and all its facets, I made a journal entry. My devotional from the Upper Room, said…. when you have done it unto the least of these… you have done it unto Me (Jesus). Tears of joy and sadness flowed as I remembered our journey. Washing her face with warm cloths, stroking her hair to comfort, making sure her needs were met to make the time as pleasant as possible, jumping up whenever she called. God's grace had carried us through, and will continue to do so always. His love released through us allows other to be released from fears. Fall was in the air and the leaves falling, and the wind blowing bringing winter with it.

Winter came. Always for me a quiet season of indoor hibernation. The early dark keeps me inside the house evenings and the cold isn't my favorite except when we have snow. I love sit by my picture window, observing the beauty of the white flakes falling on the landscape, covering everything in white. The hush as life slows down and activity lessens, makes time for reading and sewing and warm soups, all of which bring deep satisfaction. That winter I had a lot to reflect upon. Almost a year passed since Tracy and I had started our trip. She was now with Jesus and I was missing her friendship.

Spring followed bringing my gardens into bloom and calling me outside. A place of true peace and joy for me, reminding me, life comes after death, just as Winter gives way to Spring, and Summer when blooming takes over and fragrances come in waves. Plantings from many people fill my 16 beds and remind me of the help they have been to my own unfurling process. So many have planted seeds in my soul and I wonder how they felt when maybe I wasn't blooming as fast as they thought I should. But I want each one to know that I am grateful for every minute or great part that changed me into the person I am today.

Two Springs later, it's now 2008, the gardens are in the second cycle of blooms. Tulips and Iris, along with Bleeding Heart, which had faded, giving way to Lily of the Valley, along with Day Lilies, trumpeting the onset of summer. Soon the Roses will open to full release of their beauty and for me this is where I myself want to go with Jesus; into my fullness, my destiny, the purpose for which I was created. Thoughts turn to remembering a 3-day consecutive vision I recorded that Tracy had following her deliverance in California. A vision for my own hope of healing.

2-10-07 There was a beautiful garden, I was sitting on a shimmering white wrought iron settee, dressed in a long sleeve white linen dress with pretty white sandals. Jesus came and knelt in front of me. I was weeping. He took my hand and spoke. "You are my precious daughter. You know I am the King. I will never leave you or forsake you. I know your heart and dreams. The time of fulfillment is come. You have made me a footstool." Kissing my hand, He got up and reminded me again. "Remember, I will never leave you or forsake you. This garden is for you to enjoy." Then He walked away.

2-11-07 Tracy saw the garden again. This time Jesus was on the bench with a whole bunch of children clamoring around Him. He was anointing each on and saying, "Go make fishers of men." Recognizing that the children were ours, all very young. My two miscarried girls, Sarah Jane and Victoria Grace were there. Victoria had long dark brown hair and looked like her brother

Aaron. She said Sarah had mousy brown hair like my own and they both had beautiful smiles. (As she had begun telling the vision of the clamoring children, I already knew Sarah and Victoria were there among them.) She also saw her own miscarried son, Robbie. Gary and I along with Chis and Tracy were there too, walking through the gardens. Beautifully dressed and glowing with joy!

2-12-07 For the third day Tracy saw the garden. This time I was dancing with Jesus.

Remaining hopeful and patient in waiting for completeness of His work sometimes gives way to despair. But when it does, I quickly run to my Father, and he lifts me up. I have learned to trust and relish the quietness since her passing and yet only two weeks later I feel as if I barely know him, as in the beginning, questioning my faith, "Had I lost my will, my mind and my desire to minister?" Giving myself in surrender over and over, I reminded myself, He did say "in Quietness and trust, you will find me." My strength to muster up my will needed to give way to follow a new path. My need was great, and He was greater than my need. Please find me, Lord. He was hiding so I would seek Him. Trusting was a huge issue for me and to make me secure in quietness and difficulty required trusting that He is at work even if I can't always perceive it. Trust doesn't have to understand; it just says I know the character of Almighty God.

In a letter I wrote to Him, I felt his response...

Dear Susan,

I am so happy you are taking time with me. I love spending time in the gardens with you. My creation beats with the beauty of my heart for your pleasure. Listen, listen! The song is getting stronger and so are my winds You can hear me, and it is often just my presence you enjoy. No need for words. I just enjoy touching you without them. Be more aware of this and I will meet you in this way. You are so beautiful because you are free!

I never wanted my people in constraints. I love them too much to restrict them from enjoying who I created them to be. My darling this is your effect. You help people to see this enjoyment and cause them to desire it, because they have all been children and remember the wonder of childhood; the freedom of just being.

Love,
Your Father

The month following my gardens are lush and filled with God's presence. Reading from John 15:1-11 1. Jesus said I am the True Vine and my Father the vine dresser...11. I have told you these things that my joy and delight may be in you and that your joy and gladness may be of full measure, and complete and overflowing. 12. This is my commandment that you love one another just as I have loved you.

Ministering to others is easier in the experience and knowledge we personally own. Doors open for me constantly to share His love, but it took time to develop sight to see, and even skills to open the most "stuck" of them. The Fruit of the Holy Spirit, which is love, joy, peace, patience, gentleness, kindness, goodness, faithfulness, quietness and self-control are the keys to open those doors. The facets and ways of His love are never failing.

Again, the door to develop a friendship again would open and be the one that led me to the final frontiers leading to His full measure for me. Joni and I met through our children who became friends. She only lives up the hill and that too would become means for closer relationship. Her family came to PA from Louisiana in the 90's and we had begun to do things sporadically in the early 2000's. Her happy countenance and drawl drew me to our common ground: Jesus.

Not only did we work together, but small group, shopping and planning her eldest daughter's wedding would be the stuff of increased growth and blessing for both of us. She offered me a more mature friendship. Trust would come as we connected on every level and saw God using us for each other and along the path of our adventures together in other's lives.

The wedding included redecorating her house, bridal shower, brunch, reception and wedding. A monumental task that took us deep into love and care for each other and all the details to fulfilling everyone's desires for a memorable time of celebration. On a weekend trip, she said we need to get moving on the house. I asked where she wanted to start. Her reply "Well first thing I want is a mirror above my buffet. 72" x 36" with a beveled edge and a 5" in convex frame." Dollar signs were flashing in my mind and thoughts as to where to begin finding it. After trying on my own, I lifted it to prayer. Often, we just start praying and this was no exception. We were in faith, at least until she said, "Oh and I only want to pay $200!" My quick response put me back in faith, "You heard that God." Expressing that we both were excited to see how he would answer. We went on to leave it and enjoy our time together with her girls.

Wednesday following our return on Monday, I was working with a neighbor to make some draperies. My phone rang. It was Gary. "Hi, could we use a mirror, we are taking it out of a bathroom job, and they are going to throw it in the dumpster, but it is perfectly good." I was curious to know more. "What size is it?" Going he described it. "It's 72" by 36" inches and has a beveled edge." I went ballistic! He had not known about our request in prayer and now the clincher. "How much do they want?" He says, "It's free!" Then, 'YES!", it was perfect, minus the frame, but no doubt that could be remedied. I immediately called Joni, rejoicing and shouting in God's provision.

Thursday evening Gary and I went to a fellowship and worship time where we ran into Stanton and Lydia. Gary had worked for Stanton as a young man and only rarely had he seen him since. On this occasion, I was sharing the story of our mirror, as they listened intently with amazement. Finishing, Stanton says, "I can make the frame. I have all the equipment in my house basement." Again, God's unmistakable intervention made my joy complete. We decided the frame would be made to Joni's desired likeness. Gary and I painted it to match her chandelier in a metallic sponged finish and Stanton handed Joni the bill. $200! God is amazing and the room turned into Joni's vision. Giving God the credit is important. He loves to grant us our requests and appreciates our acknowledgement of His ability to provide.

God was preparing me to overcome many communication fears and to trust deeply in what he has spoken. Joni was a committed sister and friend, holding me to accountability, honesty, truth and walking together on the straight and narrow path. Walking with me through the next years she proved to be a steadying pillar needed when trials and tests came with overwhelming emotions, circumstances and required a wise, listening presence to help me see in the darkness.

My mother would pass on to heaven in 2010 and she would lose a very close friend to cancer as well. A child's betrayal, an unplanned miscarriage, a new granddaughter to bring joy to me. These were but a few of the scenarios. Empathy was ever present, and our prayers for "Thy kingdom come, thy will be done." Unearthed countless blessings and her hand extended to help me from falling, gave me a security in Christ, deeper than I had know even with Tracy.

The dark times seemed to lighten for a while and during a shopping trip to the Christian bookstore, she found a book. "You should get this, Susan. I really think you need this." The title was "The Wounded Heart/Hope for Adult victims of Childhood Sexual Abuse". I did not argue, her conviction rang true. I bought it and began to open its pages, unearthing a new healing process the Lord wanted for me. Dan Allender again. He had helped me earlier and I knew his work to be effective. The time must be right for the next stages of healing, which were never uncomplicated and painless. He offers advice to pray about unrevealed memory that could bring understanding to still lingering questions about my past. I always felt my behavior prior to my molestation at age 8 was still a mystery. Facts shrouded in darkness, covering the cause of my ever present promiscuity, a character trait, I remember having from the age of 4.

After praying the request, I trusted God to give the answer I needed whether affirming or disaffirming, He would settle me in my need for understanding. One day as I was waking from a nap on our love seat, I heard God. "Susan, do you remember when your mother told you she took you to the Doctor, at age 3 months, with bright red blood in your diaper?" I recalled suddenly that she had spoken to me about this back in the late 90's. However, that was a busy time with family and not a lot of focus on me…it had been tucked away in my memory bank and God just pulled it out. My question of why had been answered. My feelings of unsureness and restlessness were now settled. He would help me face the yet unrevealed consequences of that event. Denial, of the reality, would only serve to keep me in the cycle of abuse that started then. Exposure to light is pertinent, only then we can see clearly to overcome the shame which holds us. The statistics of sexual abuse are appalling and astounding. Dr. Allender lays out the four stages of sexual abuse.

Stage 1. Intimacy and Secrecy
"The first stage of abuse can be considered a conscious intentional set-up that opens the refrigerator doors to the sight and taste of a hungry child"

Stage 2. Physical Contact that appears appropriate
The essence of Stage 2 is the beginning of physical and sensual bonding

Stage 3. Sexual Abuse Proper.
Sexual Abuse is the final blow that sabotages the soul in a climactic betrayal, mocking the enjoyment of relationship and pouring contempt on the thrill of passion

Stage 4 Threats and Privileges
The final stage of abuse is in many ways like the first stage: the development of intimacy and secrecy. Unlike the first stage, however, the glory days are gone forever. The abuser will use whatever leverage he or she can to instill loyalty and fear in the heart of the victim to insure silence and compliance.

Including these stages may help you identify similarity in your experience, but I encourage you to read the book and do the work in the corresponding workbook. God can do miracles and will. He is a safe place and knows all the happenings of your life. He is the only one with complete understanding who can be trusted to heal your heart for Love's sake.

Love is essentially a movement of grace to embrace those who have been wounded, and those who have wounded. Matthew 5: 43-48 is the offer of restoration to those who have harmed, for the purpose of destroying evil and enhancing life. Love can be defined as the free gift that voluntarily cancels debt in order to free the debtor to become what he might be if he experiences the joy of restoration. Requiring a choice by the victim, I chose to free my abusers from their debt. That way, we all could know the joy of restoration. Our forgiveness opens the way for God to be able by His Holy Spirit to seek out and pursue the abuser to give them what we have chosen. Love and Forgiveness.

The other side of the coin, so to speak, is that we must also learn to receive love and forgiveness and do it graciously. Abuse makes us abusive to our own self. Hard expectations of oneself that continue to beat us down long into the future after the act is over. We feel unworthy of love and forgiveness. Learning to be good to ourselves frees us to live in an otherwise state apart from the tenseness of abuse. Allowing others to bless us invites goodness to come. And gives the others the reality experiencing the truth of "it is more blessed to give than to receive." No one wants to always be the giver. We all like receiving and to do it with openness brings us the desire of helping others sow seed for their own harvest.

The years of 2011 and following continued to bring great trials in my life. Another wedding and reception surrounded with turmoil and pain, a family member married 42 years and a missionary; abandoned by her husband, a return of a family member who had strayed but then left again, dashed and expectant at the same time. This is the stuff of transformation of the inner man. Sometimes it doesn't feel good. Sometimes we are looking for God and He is hidden in a dark cloud. There with us; but quiet. Sometimes we feel like we have nothing left. These are the times we go humbly seeking His presence to restore refresh and renew what the ravages of life and sin have done. Then my father passed.

The barrage of trials seemed to drain me of energy and life, stress had taken its toll. God's wisdom sustained me through it all and gave me a strong sense of his presence with me. Although attacks continued, I had the strength and grace to see me through to the other side, covered in His Love. Feeling God's love for me, motivates me to love more. The Joy of Loving fills my heart like nothing else does. Mick Jagger..." I got SATISFACTION!"

Fall arrived and the Hebrew New Year 5776. Robert Heidler, a teacher from Glory of Zion in Corinth, Texas, was teaching about the meaning and purpose God intended to give in the New Year. Ayin and Vav were the names and word representations connected to 5776 and held the meaning of the eyes of God and connecting our past to the future and our future to our past. God lives in a time circle in Eternity and wants to do this work in our lives. He can be anywhere at anytime on the circle and take us there with him spiritually.

Intrigue of possibilities lead to meditation on this concept and a desire for the new year and its application to my own personal life. I still knew my healing was not finished and this could be the answer to receiving it. Eventually, a revelation of how it could work lead me to understand that God could VAV me in time back to the time before I was 3 months old and I was still not robbed of my soul, all my God given innate abilities still intact and functioning. I know this is deep but bear with me. Only now if God chose to do this for me would I have my original ability to be the person I was created to be restored to wholeness.

I believe I was given a major key of understanding and revelation not just for me but for all those who would chose to pick it up and use it for unlocking their own healing from any traumatic circumstance that stole a part of them and thrust them out of God's peace and purpose. Proverbs 16:3 was the scripture I desired to be fulfilled in my being. "Roll your works on the Lord [commit and trust] them wholly to Him; He will cause your thoughts to become agreeable to His will and so shall your plans be established and succeed. My prayer to go deeper into His love had never failed and I understood it came with trial and test. Fear of intimacy would not hold me from surrender. I want all He has for me. Isaiah 41: 13 directed my decision; I the Lord God hold your hand, I am the Lord, who says to you "Fear Not, I will help you."

A day long women's retreat thrust me from journal to introspection and onward to revelation. I would write John Eldredge's words from his book, entitled EPIC.

"Something has been calling to me all the days of my life. I've heard it in the wind and in the music. In love, in laughter, and in tears and most especially in the stories that have captured my heart. There is a secret written on my heart. A valiant Hero-Lover and His beloved." It resonated loudly within my heart and soul. These words were the explanation of the longing in the human heart which only Christ my Hero-Lover was meant to be, The Something I heard calling, the call I needed to answer. There's that "telephone answering service" that Dave said, God wanted to put in our marriage! LOL Answer His call!

Memorial Day of 2016 I was ill. It didn't seem serious or like it would endure however I was wrong. Days then weeks passed laying in my bed unable to function in a normal routine. I ask the Lord to remember me, have mercy and restore me. Weak and needy, crying in pain, my husband cared for me when he was home on weekends. I felt God's love through him. Only after six weeks did I consider a visit to a Homeopathic Doctor whom I had met in 2009 at a fellowship I attended weekly for three years. An ASYRA test, a cellular level read of my body revealed stress, foods to be avoided, and the Holy Spirit revealed to him, unwarranted insults. His remedies were effective, and he said within a couple of days I would notice a marked sense of calm.

Not a couple of days but almost immediately I realized the connection was made. My original state of restful, peaceful, calm, thoughtful, state of being had been restored. God had VAVED me! I thanked God over and over and enjoyed the freedom from 60 years in a state of tense. That had been my "norm". Only could I see how messed up I was when Jesus came into my heart with the Light of His Spirit, shining in my darkness. Another journal entry cut from a magazine: He makes tough messes wish they were never made.

Just as Much Afraid was laid on the alter to have human love rent from her heart. The cave of her transformation was filled with sweet fragrances, spikenard, frankincense and myrrh. The wrappings which covered her emanated with their fragrance. After rising she traversed not thinking about her future. "It was enough to be there in that quiet canyon hidden away high up in the mountains with the river of life flowing beside her, and to rest and recover herself after the long journey." I was enjoying the fragrance of my bloom.

It would take months, to regain strength, and He knew that. I never was one to sit around and do nothing. I need a slower pace of life to realize and enjoy my new perspective of God. The next year He would have me revisit the foundations of Love, Grace, Mercy and so on…They would no longer look like they had in the past. I was no longer broken. I could see Gentle God. He always was Gentle, but the problem wasn't Him. It was me. Broken, Blind, Crippled, and Lost in a prison of human creation. He is God, who wants to eradicate the effect of not only my sin, but the sin of the whole world. HE LOVES YOU!!!!!!!!

My Journey with my Hero-Lover lives on forever. While the enemy deceives, robs, kills and destroys, I will be a weapon in the hand of my Lover and Lord to do good through His Love. Not one is untouched by sin and the enemy, yet the answers remain available.

Without His perspective our world is hopeless to help. His willingness does not stop this side of eternity. Do you want his Love to change your Life?

No matter where he allows you to go, there will be opportunity to share who he is and his relevant Life changing relationship. Love flows like a river after a heavy rain watering soul and spirit to bring water to the thirsty and desperate. Imagine a neighborhood, town or nation as that river increases to bring refreshment and you can say, "I am part of the River of Life."

The river flows wherever it pleases, and the wind blows wherever as well. You feel the refreshment and hear it's sound, but you cannot tell where it comes from or where it is going. So, it is with everyone born of the Spirit. I love the River, with all its sometimes calm, sometimes white water, and always beautiful vistas. It's can be a wild ride at times, but God is always with us when we invite Him on the ride! With man it is impossible, but with God all things are possible. I just want to say thank you to my Father, the Son and Holy Spirit who say through Joseph in Genesis 50:20 AMP "As for you, you meant evil against me, but God meant it for good in order to bring this present outcome, that many people would be kept alive [as they are this day]."

Epilogue

I missed my mom this week. Not often do I linger to think longingly of her other than special dates, but this season God has nudged me. Looking at old photos she saved, and I inherited. Her birthday is not long past, September 30. God is reminding me of her own beauty. Her picture with phone in hand, a snorky smile and youthful, playful image is my favorite. Showing me a side and season of her life witnessed only in rare occasions during my own adult years. I am extremely grateful to be a keeper of these treasures dating back 80 plus years. Portraying a view of a young woman yet unburdened by the responsibilities of marriage motherhood. Moments of lighthearted fun dissipated into the tasks and duties that filled her days. I had not witnessed these moments, for they had slipped off the pages of her story, landing on the hard reality of all her life entailed as daughter, wife, mother, sister and friend. Her smile faded and became less. Her reply upon the question, "How are you? "was "Surviving, able to take food and nourishment." Smiling became harder as circumstances forced her to keep on without realizing what she carried on the inside. Then a great loss, a son, the one who was thankful and expressed it. She had prepared three meals a day for her family and they were most delicious. The best of the best.

One of her bests was homemade applesauce. I guess that me making applesauce continued stirring thoughts of her. I thought the only way to make applesauce was mom's way and since I have given up sugar, I haven't made it much. But last week, my second cousin, Earl, blessed us from his harvest of Jona Gold, Golden delicious and Red Delicious (only for eating). His wife, Cindy, had mixed the two Gold to make a naturally sweet applesauce. New idea to me, but it opened the door to enjoy making applesauce once again. My children chided, "You better have some when I come for Christmas!" I laughed, happy to oblige!

And tonight, when skyping with my daughter, I thought of another photo that showed a much later image of that light-hearted mom. There she was standing inside a molded dinosaur with her face smiling through his mouth, making us laugh. Naming her I said Look it's Granosaurus and Hannah replied "Gram-o-suraus" LOLOL!

Realizing the ability to appreciate, people many years after hurt and pains are healed by Jesus. A new perspective opens itself in the pages of the story. A perspective of peace rising from the depths of your soul, replacing memories. Allowing What was good to come forth. Good was always there, I was blind to see, because understanding forgiveness is freedom and freedom is peace with God and peace with others and mostly peace with your life; Who you were intended to be. There is room in the world for all of us. NO Competition, each unique in identity, giftings and purpose. THAT is the amazing Grace God planned. Grace extended to others allows freedom to Be. No Pressure to be conformed to the world only grace to be. Conformed into the image of Christ, a true son or daughter who love to please Father God, who waits for our heart to be willing to perceive His loving forgiveness and sacrifice in the gift of Jesus. He left home, to come into a cruel sinful world where he suffered abuses common among men but remained sinless. Forgiveness is the key which kept him free and forgiveness is the reason he took our sin to the cross. Only He had the power to overcome sin, hell, death and the grave and offer it to the world for free, in order to restore relationship with His creation. To Save, rescue and restore us to life in his Kingdom forever. He Is God and He is Good. Go after His heart! You will not be disappointed.

www.ingramcontent.com/pod-product-compliance
Lightning Source LLC
Chambersburg PA
CBHW030922090426
42737CB00007B/287